In the Land

Of

Joys and Sorrows

Our Life in Burundi

Ivar Serejski

Innovations & Information, Inc
http://www.iandi.cc

In the Land of Joys and Sorrows

Editions Innovations and Information, Inc.
Frederick, MD 21702
http://www.iandi.cc

© October 30, 2013 by Ivar Serejski
All rights reserved. Published 2013
Published in the United States of America
18 17 16 15 14 13   5 4 3 2 1

All rights reserved. No part of this document may be reproduced, transmitted, transcribed, stored in a retrieval system, transmitted in any form, or translated into any language by any means (electronically, mechanically, photocopied, recorded, etc.) without the prior written permission of the publisher or author.

The information and views in this book are those of the author alone. Nevertheless, the author and the publisher cannot be held responsible for any error or omission. They also cannot be held responsible for views expressed based on the information contained in this book.

Edited by Frédérique Duverger
Published by Eric Serejski

ISBN 978-0-9853477-4-1

Author's Note

I have modified most of the names of the persons cited in order to maintain their anonymity.

In the Land of Joys and Sorrows

Acknowledgements

With all my heart, I thank Eric Serejski, my publisher, for his professional advice. I also thank Frédérique Duverger, my editor and Mrs. Michèle De Coninck for authorizing me to use the photos of her website. For my wife Nadine, my children Eric and Karin, and all those who have maintained my thirst to tell.

In the Land of Joys and Sorrows

Table of Contents

Table of Contents 7
FOREWORD xi
I. PREPARATIONS FOR DEPARTURE 13
   When I Was a City-Dweller 13
   Our Wedding 16
   The Adventures of Johnny 16
II. DEPARTURE TO BURUNDI 19
   Brussels Airport (Zaventem) 19
   Athens 19
   Entebbe (Uganda) 20
III. BURUNDI 23
   The Land of Sacred Drums 23
   History: 1899-1962 25
   Geography 25
   The Demographic and Political Contexts 26
   Bujumbura 26
IV. TEZA 29
   First Trip in the Bush 29
   Our Lodge 31
   Settling In 33
   First Contact with my Working Universe 35
   From the City to the Bush, From Theory to Practice 36
   A Terrible Tragedy 39
   The Inauguration of the Rural Clinic 40
   An Ongoing Challenge 42
   The Batwas and the Hunt 48
   A Freak Accident 49
   The Family Grows 50
   Visits of the Mwami 52
   The Bushmen Go Into Town 53
   Our Move 56
   The Ambush 57
   The Wedding of My Burundian Friend 58
   The Dreadful Carbon Monoxide 61
   Religious Festivals 62
V. A LONG ESCAPADE 63
   Our Trip to East Africa 63
   Akagera Park 64
   Initial Contact with Uganda 65
   Murchison Falls National Park 66
   En route to Kenya and Tanzania 69

From Masai Mara to Kilimanjaro 70
Eric the Explorer 71
From Kilimanjaro to Nairobi 72
The Long Way Home 73
VI. THE OCTOBER 1965 COUP 75
The Beginnings of the Coup 75
The Coup in Bujumbura 75
The Massacre of Tutsis in Teza 76
A Risky Gamble 82
My Daily Visits to Teza 85
The Gruesome Discovery 86
The Premonition 87
A Gradual Return to Normal 89
VII. BACK TO THE PLANTATION 91
Another Challenge 91
Political Developments 92
We are Four 93
Intuition 96
The Mimic Gift of Monkeys 97
The Flight over the Plantation in DC3 102
Our Hunting Night in the Province of Kirundo 103
New Attempt or Simulacrum of a Coup 108
VIII. BUJUMBURA 111
My New Assignment 111
First Contact with the United States 112
Tanganyika Lake 114
My Dives in the Lake 115
The Crocodile, a Constant Danger 118
IX - THE GENOCIDE OF 1972 123
The Context 123
The Massacre of Hutus 123
I Listen to My Conscience 125
X. POST GENOCIDE 129
The Duty to Remember 129
The Philanthropic Club and the Traffic Lights 132
President Micombero, a Foosball Game Passionate 133
The Driver without a Vehicle 134
My Passion for Rugby 135
My Return to Burundi 136
My Hunt in the Mosso Plain 137
Our Last Trip to the Virunga National Park 140
XI. A FEW YEARS LATER 147
A Different Immersion 147
Lake Cyohoha 147

 I Hang Around with Hippos 149
 And Not Only Hippos.. 151
 My Reunion with Nicolas... 151
 The Confrontation of Two Perspectives 153
XII. A RETURN TO THE ROOTS... 155
 Why This Book 155
 Bujumbura 158
 The Problem of Corruption 163
 My Visits in the Country Side 164
 Issues of the Return of Refugees 177
 Security Issues 178
XIII. EPILOGUE... 181
ANNEX. LAKE TANGANYIKA 185
 The Context.. 185
 Wildlife 185
 The Pelagic Community 186
 Sublittoral and Littoral Communities 186
 Aquatic and Terrestrial Species 187
Bibliography.. 189
 Authors... 189
 Other Sources... 191

In the Land of Joys and Sorrows

FOREWORD

September 1960. The academic year is about to start at the University Faculty of Agricultural Sciences of Gembloux, Belgium, where I just finished two years of my Bachelor's Degree. I was at a crossroads in my life, as I had to make a final selection amongst different Master's Degrees. I decided to undertake a Master's Degree in Tropical Agriculture, which was the only degree offering the possibilities to fulfill my dream and work abroad. At that time, expatriation was generally associated with an assignment either in the Congo[1] or in the two countries still under Belgian rule, namely the actual Burundi and Rwanda. For many of us, expatriation was a very attractive choice when we began our studies in 1958. However, this option was almost abandoned in 1960, given the climate of insecurity that began before the proclamation of independence of Belgian Congo on June 30, 1960, including the riots in Leopoldville[2] in 1959, fueled by the inflammatory speeches of Patrice Lumumba. The police mutiny on the day of independence and the secession of Katanga on July 11, 1960 only exacerbated the precarious political situation. Looting, riots, rapes, and killings became daily events in a Congo that, becoming independent, slid inexorably toward a climate of chaos, savagery and murder. There was a total scission between Belgium and the Congo. In this adverse environment, the best professional future for Agricultural Master's Degree holders wishing to pursue a career overseas became quite uncertain and risky. Yet, like six of my fellow students, I did not want a sanitized career without surprises in Belgium and remained attracted by the unknown and challenges, as well as the need to provide assistance to developing countries. To achieve this goal, we all decided to start our Master's Degrees in Tropical Agriculture. I have never regretted my choice.

---

[1] I use the term 'Congo' to refer to the contemporary Democratic Republic of Congo (DRC), name used since May 1997. I use the term 'Zaire' to refer to the same country under the regime of Joseph Désiré Mobutu (1965-1997).
[2] Known as Kinshasa since 1966.

In the Land of Joys and Sorrows

I. PREPARATIONS FOR DEPARTURE

When I Was a City-Dweller

September 1963. I was 23 and finishing my Master's Degree in Tropical Agriculture at the University Faculty of Agricultural Sciences of Gembloux, Belgium. My dream was about to be realized, I hoped. I always wanted to go abroad, to travel, to discover the African continent I knew only through books, and to contribute to its development while practicing Agronomy. Ironically, I was a pure city-dweller with no practical experience in Agronomy, but it did not matter! At the time, hiring was not a concern.

Tropical Agriculture was no longer popular since the tragic events that had bereaved the Congo after its independence in 1960. Massacres, rapes and looting did little to encourage students to pursue studies in this area. Only seven of us were graduating with this specialty and employment; for those who wanted to emigrate, should not have theoretically posed any problems.

After the results were announced in September 1963, a colleague of mine who got his Master's Degree in 1961 and was working at the faculty, told me that two positions just opened up in Burundi might interest me. Thanks to this friendly tip, I strolled into the faculty's corridors with one of my best friends and stopped in front of the panel job. Among the numerous offers, two were indeed for Burundi, which seemed much more reassuring and less dangerous than the Congo. The Institute of Agronomic Sciences of Burundi (ISABU) was recruiting two Master's Degree holders in Tropical Agriculture. The first position to be filled was for a Plant Pathologist in the headquarters of ISABU in Bujumbura, whereas the second one was for an Agriculturalist who would be responsible for establishing the first 1,250 acres tea plantations in the forest of Burundi. My friend and I debated the offers and we quickly agreed. He chose Plant Pathology and I opted for the tea position. Though growing tea was completely unknown to me and my book knowledge was rather rudimentary, I was all agog for such a challenge and decided to take the plunge.

We thus contacted the Belgian headquarters of ISABU, Avenue Louise in Brussels, to make an appointment. At the beginning of October 1963, I met with the General Director of ISABU, a Belgian, whom I will call Alfred, and who had spent his entire career in Africa, especially in the Congo, Rwanda and Burundi. Alfred was a very impressive corpulent person, with a voice that nobody could mistake. He quickly questioned me about my reasons to work abroad and, after ten minutes of conversation, asked me if I could be in Burundi within ten days! I could not believe my ears and had difficulties realizing that ten days later, I might be in Burundi. However, such a quick departure raised a serious dilemma. Indeed, I wanted to get married before leaving Belgium. Therefore, a period of ten days, to me, seemed very inadequate to complete logistic, administrative and health formalities and to get married before my expatriation. To test the waters, I explained to Alfred that I might require more than ten days getting ready; however, I did not raise the issue of my marriage, which was the main reason for a suggested delayed departure. Frowning, he replied that there should be no problem because its administrative service would take care of all formalities with the Burundian authorities and that I should only take care of my passport, medical examination and vaccines. He also offered me an advance on my salary to let me buy what was needed for my stay in Burundi. Indeed, after completing my studies, I was totally broke. Falling short of arguments, I disclosed my secret, and told him I wanted to get married before leaving. I thought he was having an attack. He turned red, and retorted angrily that the position he had proposed to me was not appropriate for a couple because the assignment was in the bush where living conditions would be extremely difficult. He told me that for a while I was going to live in a lodge without regular running water and a few hours of electricity per day. He said that a woman, a city-dweller, moreover, could never get used to living in such harsh conditions. He added that the position needed to be filled as soon as possible and that if I were not immediately available, he would find someone else. I thought the sky was falling on my head! I tried to reassure him that I would do everything possible to break the banns to get married quickly, and that he should not worry about Nadine, my future wife, as I was sure that she would adapt to the bush-living conditions. In fact, I was speaking without knowing Nadine's reaction. I was wondering what she would say when I would mention to her that we had to marry before the end of October, leave Belgium and our respective parents soon after our marriage and live in the bush, that neither one of us knew. I guess that my future Director was convinced with my explanations as he proposed me to sign a two-year contract with the provision that I would be in Burundi no later that the 10th of November. I signed the contract without any hesitation and received an advance on my salary of several thousand Belgian Francs, which was a fortune compared to what I was used to during my studies. Indeed, at that time I was living with about four thousand Belgian Francs per month[3]. I had a contract, I had money, I was going to get married soon and everything seemed idyllic. Of course, I was far from suspecting the living conditions that were awaiting us and the strange adventures and misadventures that we would be facing.

I went home and announced, not without apprehension, that I just signed a contract with ISABU to fulfill a managing position for a tea plantation in Burundi, and that I should be in the country within 20 days. I explained to Nadine that my assignment would be in the bush, where I would be responsible for establishing the first tea plantation in Burundi. I added that my contract was for a renewable period of two years, with a return to Belgium at the end of this period, which meant that we could not see our parents and friends before 24 months! We would both be confronted with the harsh reality of expatriation and the unknown. To date, 50 years later after telling Nadine about our imminent departure, I still do not realize how she could have accepted with such composure to leave everything and travel to Africa, in a distant land we did not know.

The race against time began. First, I had to inform my future in-laws and my parents of our decision to break the banns in order to obtain a dispensation and get married as soon as possible. Then, we had to complete a series of administrative formalities and medical exams including a series of vaccinations, shop for our stay in Africa, and organize our wedding and our departure. We completed everything within 20 days, not without adventures, but

---

[3] The Belgian Franc (BEF) is obsolete. It was replaced with the Euro (EUR) on January 1, 1999. One EUR is equivalent to 40.3399 BEF. In 1963, one US$ was equivalent to 50 BEF.

the adventures would be part of our lives throughout the eleven years of our stay in Burundi and during my subsequent ones.

Our Wedding

October 30, 1963. After breaking the banns, we were civilly married at Grand Place's City Hall in Brussels. In my haste, I almost forgot to buy the bridal bouquet! Back at home, the feast began. My mother, always looking for original ideas, offered us as a wedding gift a three-year-old male boxer, Johnny. She knew that since childhood I always had a passion for dogs. Like us, Johnny was a city-dweller and his universe was limited to staying in a provincial dyeing place for three years. Between the latter, the long flight to Burundi and the bush waiting for him, the margin was great. Nevertheless, before leaving, he took part in the wedding party and learned to know the streets of Brussels. So here he was, mingling with guests, placing his long lips on the evening dresses and costumes. With joy ruling, his friendly behavior went rather unnoticed, I think. Or was it just an impression? The party was in full swing when suddenly the telephone rang. At the other end of the line, my future director, Alfred, asked me to take a delivery of twelve piglets in Zaventem, Brussels Airport, the day we were to leave. I thought of course that it was a joke, a hoax. This was not the case, and my agricultural journey began even before boarding. We were going to board the flight to Bujumbura with a 90 pounds dog and twelve piglets. For a city-dweller, the beginning of my career could not be better!

The Adventures of Johnny

With the party over and our friends gone, the adventures of Johnny were just beginning. The next day I took him for a walk on the road of Charleroi in Brussels, where the circulation of cars and streetcars was particularly dense. Feeling that he was obedient, I removed his leash, as I always did with my dogs. The beginning was perfect and he followed me like my shadow on the sidewalk. However, suddenly one of his fellows strolling on the opposite sidewalk attracted his attention. Listening only to his instincts, our

Johnny crossed the road without looking left or right. I called him but to no avail. Suddenly, the drama occurred. At full speed, Johnny weighing about 90 pounds hit the rear fender of a car. Projected into the air, he fell back onto his feet and joined the other side of the road. I rushed to see if he was injured. To my great relief, he seemed unharmed, which was later confirmed by a veterinarian friend. The problem was not Johnny, but the car, whose driver had stopped. The driver asked me how my dog was doing and then, pointing to his heavily damaged fender, told me that I would have to take over the repair of his vehicle. I did not know what to say because I was penniless. Seeing my distress, he asked me if I had a car. I nodded because I actually had an old Morris Minor from 1950. It served me during my studies and I was about to sell it. He told me that the repair would not be a problem as long as I declared that the accident happened with my car. To formalize our agreement, I signed a paper acknowledging the facts and we parted. He was satisfied and I was relieved! Yes, people were less complicated and more understanding at the time.

In the Land of Joys and Sorrows

II. DEPARTURE TO BURUNDI

Brussels Airport (Zaventem)

November 5, 1963. Here we were in Zaventem, bound for Burundi. Our twelve piglets were waiting for us. In the registration line, some people looked at us quite aback. Indeed, travelling with twelve piglets and a dog was rather unusual! Johnny, as suggested by my veterinarian friend, had received a tranquilizer for his trip. Baggage, living and nonliving, were recorded without any problems and we took place on the DC7 of Sabena,[4] whose multiple stops itinerary would take us to Bujumbura via Athens, Cairo and Entebbe. In the plane, I dreamed of Africa and was skimming through the many documents I had been entrusted with, including a very serious book on tropical hygiene.[5] I found words such as malaria, filariasis, schistosomiasis, which reminded me of my hygiene course I followed at the Faculty. I must admit, however, that I did not pay too much attention to the latter courses while attending the University. Suddenly, I began to attach some importance to these medical words. Still, I did not realize then that these tropical and sub-tropical diseases would gradually be part of the difficulties that we were going to face in our bush life.

Athens

After several hours, the plane landed in Athens. Everyone disembarked for a first stop of about an hour and a half. There was more than enough time to go quietly take a snack in the cafeteria of the airport. Of course, I thought of my dog and, without paying too much attention to the effect of the tranquilizer

---

[4] Belgian national airline, which closed in 2001.
[5] Duren, A.; Gillet, H. *Notions élémentaires d'hygiène tropicale à l'usage des habitants du Congo Belge*. [Basics of Tropical Hygiene for use by residents of the Belgian Congo]

he had received before boarding, I asked the captain if I could get him off the dock so that he could stretch and eat like us. The captain did not see any problem in opening the dock. And yes, in another time, there were different safety rules. Customs baggage examinations did not exist and boarding on a plane was like going on a bus today. The ground staff then opened the dock and brought the cage down. Here was our Johnny, asleep with his tranquilizer, putting his paws on the tarmac. My good heart had taken over the logic since it would have been better to let him doze, as we shall see later. When we were in the cafeteria, I ordered him water and a sandwich, which not only satisfied him, but also brought him out of his drowsiness. We then put him back in his cage and took off for Cairo where a technical stop was planned. All passengers remained on board. Next, we headed to Entebbe where Africa was waiting for us.

Entebbe (Uganda)

The plane landed at the Entebbe airport, rolled on the tarmac for a few minutes and then stopped. The passengers were supposed to disembark but the authorization was not coming. Five minutes passed and then the captain made a call. I listened with one ear and then suddenly I heard that I was requested at the front of the plane. I got up and walked to the cockpit where the captain was waiting for me. He said that there was a serious problem with our dog. He told me that the staff on the ground opened the baggage hold and then suddenly fled for no apparent reason, shouting "simba, simba" which means lion in Kiswahili![6] The captain further said that the dog had broken the door of his cage, which had been relocated at the front of the hold in Athens, and had managed to move his head and neck through the hole in the door. Upon opening the hold, the African staff was face-to-face with him and, seeing only the head of the boxer, thought it was a lion. All of them ran away! The captain therefore kindly asked me to go down, retrieve my dog and go with him in the waiting room until his cage could be repaired. I expected the worst and could not help laughing, imagining the burlesque scene on the tarmac. Nadine and I got off the plane followed by all other passengers and

---

[6] Kiswahili is a Bantu language spoken by different ethnic groups living mainly along the coasts from northern Kenya to northern Mozambique and the Comoros Islands. Kiswahili is the official language of Kenya and Tanzania.

we headed to the cafeteria with Johnny. The poor dog, however, had his jaw bloodied because he lost three teeth in his conflict with the screen door of his cage. However, he recovered quickly from his adventure, sandwich and water helping. Still, the boarding dragged on and waiting became difficult. The heat was moist and stifling and the fans were not working. We were already confronted with the reality of African life. An hour later, Johnny's cage was fixed and we took off to our final destination, Bujumbura. As far as I know, none of the passengers knew the real reason for the delay that was attributed to technical reasons! The truth would of course be very funny to talk about but I did not know if all passengers would have appreciated it!

In the Land of Joys and Sorrows

III. BURUNDI

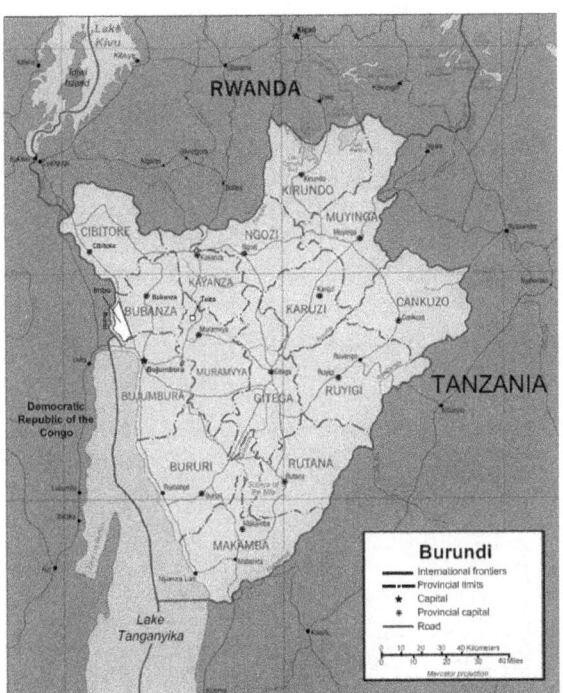

Burundi

The Land of Sacred Drums

Since immemorial time, the drums have played a key role in Burundian culture. In ancient Burundi, they symbolized the royal legitimacy and sustainability of the nation. According to a legend, a snake drumming on a cow skin stretched over a termite mound greeted the first Burundian King Ntare Rushatsi, in the 16th century. In ancient times, sacred drums were considered more than just musical instruments. They were, in fact part, of the sacred objects and were played in exceptional circumstances.

Their beat proclaimed the great events of the country, such as enthronement or funerals of sovereigns.

The Burundi monarchy used seven sacred drums, of which three are of particular importance. The first is called *nyabuhoro* and its function was to ensure that the state be secured. The second, *karyenda*, characterized the royal power. A servant known as *mukakaryenda*, or woman of *karyenda*, was responsible for its maintenance. The third, *rukinzo*, accompanied the king on his travels and was used as a clock in the sacred court. Until the end of 1966, the date of the disappearance of the Kingdom of Burundi and its replacement by a republic, the drum adorned the flag of Burundi. In contemporary Burundi, the drum remains a revered and popular instrument. Drums are present during national holidays, weddings and when receiving important guests. In Burundi, drum and kingdom have the same name: *ingoma*. There is still a network of drum sanctuaries today called the *Ingoro y'ingoma* or 'palace of the drums.'

Drums used during a wedding

History: 1899-1962

Burundi and Rwanda became part of the German East Africa in 1899 when the German settlement expansion in Africa was at its peak. In 1916, during World War I, Belgian forces in the former Belgian Congo defeated the Germans and occupied Burundi and Rwanda. In 1923, Belgium accepted the mandate of the League of the United Nations to administer Rwanda and Burundi. Both countries were administered as a single territory known as Ruanda-Urundi. In 1946, these territories were entrusted to the Trusteeship Council of the United Nations with Belgian administration. Urundi became independent on July 1, 1962 as the Kingdom of Burundi and King (Mwami) Mwambutsa IV Bangiricenge assured power. Rwanda became independent on the same day.

Geography

Burundi is a landlocked country located in the rift of Central Africa, its geographic coordinates are 3 ° 30 S, and 30°0' E (see Map p. 23). It covers an area of 10,745 miles,² of which 841 miles are of water. The north east of Lake Tanganyika, which borders the country for 93 miles, represents 95% of the water surface. The remaining 5% consists of rivers and the Cyohoha and Rweru lakes in the north. Burundi also has the particularity of being situated on the watershed of two river basins: the Nile basin opening into the Mediterranean Sea to the northeast, and the Congo River basin opening into the Atlantic Ocean to the west. Contemporary neighboring countries are the Democratic Republic of Congo, Rwanda and Tanzania. Burundi is a country of highlands with marked altitude differences, ranging from 2,530 to 8,760 feet and has an equatorial climate tempered by altitude. The average annual temperature ranges between 62.6 and 73.4°F. Annual rainfalls average 4.9 feet and are mainly distributed in two rainy seasons, the most important stretches from February to May, while the second extends from mid-October to early January. The rustic appearance and physical beauty of the country have also significantly marked the first European explorers who called it "Switzerland of Africa" and "Mountains of the Moon."

The Demographic and Political Contexts

Burundi had a population of approximately 8.3 million people in 2010 and the density of inhabitants/km² is one of the highest in the world.[7] There are three ethnic groups, the Hutu (Bantu) representing 85% of the population, the Tutsi (Hamitic) representing 14%, and the Batwas representing 1%. The Pygmies were the first inhabitants of the Great Lakes region that have lived much as they live now for the past several thousand years.[8] They are related to other communities throughout the Congo commonly referred to as Pygmies, a term that the Batwas reject as derogatory. The Hutus probably arrived in the region of the Great Lakes[9] in the 11th century and subdued the Pygmies until the arrival of the Tutsis of Nilotic origin who probably migrated from Ethiopia in the 13th century.[10] Burundi has known for long periods of time many ethnic strives and social conflicts. This situation hindered the citizens' wellbeing and the socio-economic development. The genesis of this turmoil dates back to feudal times when the divine right monarchy imposed serfdom and nepotism as an essential foundation of power. While many citizens oppressed by the feudal monarchy had placed high hopes for changes, the constitutional monarchy established by Mwambutsa IV during the political independence on July 1, 1962 did not significantly alter the social relations between ethnic groups.

Bujumbura

November 10, 1963. The DC7 landed on the tarmac of the airport of Bujumbura. It was midday, the sun at the zenith shone on a sky sprinkled with clouds and the atmosphere was heavy and wet. We were at the beginning of the rainy season. Many onlookers were waiting for the plane because, as we learned later, the biweekly arrival of the plane from Brussels was always an event.

---

[7] The World Bank; Burundi - Data & Statistics. *Burundi at a glance.*
[8] Gates, Henry Louis. *Africana,* p. 338.
[9] The region of the Great Lakes is a geopolitical entity shaped from north to south by a chain of lakes forming natural boundaries between the countries around them: the Democratic Republic of Congo (DRC, formerly Zaire), Uganda, Rwanda, Burundi and Tanzania, all populated by many ethnic groups.
[10] There are at least four theories about these origins. See Wikipedia *Origins of Tutsi and Hutu.*

After having picked our numerous luggage sets, our piglets and our faithful Johnny, we were greeted by the accountant of the ISABU, Henri. He took us to the hotel Paguidas,[11] the best hotel at the time, though it was already very tired. Henri suggested to rest because the next day it was planned that my director Alfred and I would go familiarize myself with my future workplace at Teza and our housing conditions. However, he asked me to come alone for this first contact. I did not ask too many questions, but understood later the strategy that was behind organizing this trip without Nadine. In the evening, I led Johnny in the kitchens of the hotel so that he could eat. This was certainly the first time that the staff of the premises saw a boxer and they nicknamed him Simba, or Lion as the ground employees had already done during the landing at Entebbe. In the kitchen, I heard only laughter and derision, which is generally abhorred by dogs. However, Johnny appeared neither vindictive nor aggressive during this first meeting. After two days, however, upset by the attitudes of the local staff, his attitude changed completely and he would become extremely irritable towards Africans.

The legendary Hotel Paguidas
(Picture: Courtesy of Michèle De Coninck)

---

[11] The Hotel Paguidias, of colonial architecture, had been for a long time the center of activities in Bujumbura. At the end of the last century, it was razed and replaced by the Novotel Bujumbura. In 2010, the Novotel Bujumbura was taken by the Hilton Hotel.

In the Land of Joys and Sorrows

IV. TEZA

First Trip in the Bush

November 11, 1963. That day marked my first contact with Teza[12] where we would live for seven years. Teza is located 7,218 feet above sea level on the Congo-Nile Crest.[13] 34.2 miles separates it from Bujumbura. At the time, this distance consisted in 21.7 miles of paved road, 9.3 miles of severely degraded dirt road and 3.1 miles of track. Many asphalt sections had gone away by frequent landslides. The asphalt road was very steep and went from 2,297 feet (altitude of Lake Tanganyika) to 7,500 feet in 21.7 miles. Turns succeeded to turns and precipices to precipices. The scenery was enchanting and consisted of well-separated hills. The hill, or *umusozi*,[14] is a concept as much social as geographical for Burundians. It is the smallest geographical unit of measurement and contains 100 to 150 habitations, mostly huts. Each hut is built of adobe and covered with a thatched roof and is generally surrounded by a wall of Euphorbia and bordered by banana trees. Homes built in more durable materials with metal roofing were rare. Some banana plantations could be found here and there encircling the entrance of a small kraal. Nearby one would sometimes find a field of small crops, cassava, beans, squash, or a coffee plantation, where, with the so typical peasant pace, some farmers were hoeing, digging and weeding.

---

[12] Formerly known as Nyabigondo from the name of a river bordering the forest surrounding the future tea plantation.
[13] The Congo-Nile Crest is a prominent north-south ridge reaching an altitude of at least 8,530 feet above sea level and forming the watershed area of the Nile and the Congo.
[14] The term "colline" is preferred to "hill" because it refers to an institutional entity that coincides with a particular hill; it delineates a community headed by a chief "de colline." The "colline" is the basic unit of government. As a result, internal mobility of rural people is difficult, and it is not uncommon to observe a coexistence of perpetrators and victims of intertribal warfare. This cohabitation also seems to be unique in the history of genocides.

After traveling 21.7 miles, we arrived at Bugarama where the famous Congo-Nile Crest begins. Bugarama, located at an altitude of 7,500 feet was immersed in a thick fog as was often the case during our stay and the temperature was cool and did not exceed 59°F. We then headed north taking the dirt road. The left side of the road was marked by the forest and its right side showed huts that dotted the area, as there are no villages in Burundi. I experienced an exhilarating feeling of having entered this paradise of beauty and sweetness. After about 6.2 miles, we came to a stall of fresh vegetables carefully lined up against the rock and refreshed by a source of water flowing from the mountain. This magical place known as the Kavumu Spring became our central supply of fresh vegetables.

Yet I also will keep a macabre souvenir of this place, as the pure water of the mountain was one day tinged with red in the dramas that we knew in 1965 and that I relate in Chapter VI. After 9.3 miles of rutted road, we turned left and travelled for 3.1 miles on a trail lined with eucalyptus trees. Then we turned left on another track ending a few hundred yards later by an expansion bordered with a house built of schist and a lodge. At a distance of about 1.2 miles, we could see the Kibira forest, this majestic secondary forest that extends to Rwanda and that would be our world for seven years.

Kavumu Spring

Our Lodge

We got out of our car and headed to the stone house where Robert lived with his wife, Maria. Robert, a Belgian agronomist and former Para-commando in the Congo, would be my colleague for seven years. After a warm welcome, Robert took us to our future home. This was a nice euphemism since the house was, in reality, a typical lodge at the time of the colonies used to host the territorial agents for a few days, in rather rudimentary conditions. The lodge built in country shale's was characterized by thick 31.5-inch walls and with the total absence of windows. My manager did not teach me anything new when he told me that life would obviously not be easy at the beginning of our stay due to the complete lack of comfort. He added that I should prepare my wife for these temporary difficulties. He then added reassuringly, that the construction of permanent houses on the plantation site would begin shortly and that we should be able to move in one of them within six months. The reality would be very different and we stayed in our lodge for 18 months. When I entered into it, I understood immediately why my manager wanted this first visit to be without Nadine. The lodge first consisted of a tiny room without windows, which would force us to keep the door open during the day to have a little light, provided it did not rain. The ensuing privacy was truly exceptional! This room, which served both as a dining room and as a living room, was equipped with a small chimney as the only source of heat. In extension of this locale was another room that served as a kitchen. The latter was equipped with a rudimentary wood stove and a canteen trunk containing the bare minimum in terms of dishes. During colonial times, the territorial agents who moved in the bush for rather long periods used these canteen trunks. On the other hand, there was no fridge in the lodge! That beats everything! It was at that moment that I realized for the first time that the direction of the ISABU in Bujumbura cared little for the well-being of expatriates living in the bush. ISABU's managers needed to comply with the financial resources allocated to them for implementing the tea project for which I was engaged and the accounting department welcomed any savings. It seemed that the latter believed, however, that it was possible to live without a fridge in the bush where we did not have any other option than to buy perishable food for an average of fifteen days. Indeed, we were only allowed to get fresh supplies in Bujumbura twice a month! Our first purchase was of course a kerosene refrigerator since electricity was just for memory.

Coming back to the general setup, the back door of the kitchen faced a Eucalyptus forest. To the left of our living room was another room. It also had no windows and was dark as a cellar. It became our bedroom! There was no door between the living room and the bedroom. In place of a door, we used a curtain. From our bedroom, three steps led down to another room. This would be our bathroom, if such a dark room devoid of windows could be called a bathroom. As for equipment, there were a bathtub and a sink recently installed. The conditions were rather stark. As for the toilet, there was none in the house. We had to go out by the kitchen door, and walk a hundred feet away to find the outdoor toilet. In addition, the subtropical rain, intense and frequent, would make this short trip rather enjoyable.

If by day such walk in nature was tolerable, by night such walk, with an oil lamp as the only source of light, was hardly idyllic as encounters with spiders and cockroaches reaching up to 2 inches in length were more than numerous.

As for the water supply to our lodge, it came from a 53-gallon gasoline drum converted into a tank and placed on the roof of the house. To feed the water tank, a truck with a trailer tank was coming back and forth as regularly as possible between the river Nyabigondo located about half a mile in the bottom of the valley and our lodge. Then, the water was brought to the roof in buckets carried by workers and then poured into the tank. Every day, in order to have hot water the guardian of the house was making a fire in the brick fireplace built under the tank. As for the power supply, it came from a rather tired old generator dating from before the Second World War. Savings were really at the forefront of ISABU's accountant. After this contact with our future home, we headed back to Bujumbura where Nadine was waiting impatiently to know my impressions. I was, however, full of dark thoughts, fearing that Nadine would refuse to live in such austere conditions and decide to return to Belgium. So I tried to prepare her as well as I could to the shock that she would necessarily feel upon discovering our future residence, but also to the life in the bush, isolated from everything except our neighbors. At first, I thought it would be especially unwise that I scare her by describing the lodge as I had seen. I told her then that the living conditions were fairly basic but that I thought it was best she judged them herself. Therefore, I did not enter into the details of the blueprint of the lodge. Instead, I decided to proceed in stages of awareness by showing her different African homes more rustic than our lodge when we would take the road to Teza. This moment of preparation and education was for me a key test for our young married life.

Settling In

Three days after our arrival in Bujumbura, we took the road to Teza. Nadine was surprised by the degree of poverty of the population and the hardiness of the homes we were crossing and could not help asking me some questions about our future home. A big word, I thought, to describe a rural lodge. As we passed a small house built with local bricks and with an iron roof, then another one, slightly more sophisticated, I told her that our future lodge was similar to this type of construction. Silence in the car. Then, after Bugarama, we drove for half an hour on the dirt road, followed by the track and finally arrived in front of our lodge. I was astonished by the reaction of Nadine. She exclaimed that this lodge was acceptable because she had expected a more rustic construction similar to those I had shown on the way. My preparatory job of presenting potential houses along the road turned out to be a success. To my amazement, Nadine adapted to our rustic living conditions remarkably.

The Lodge

The Lodge

Johnny, the guardian of the lodge

We barely had time to take possession of our lodge when a Burundian in his twenties came to us. He declared that his name was Joseph and that he would be available to serve us as a houseboy.[15] Joseph had completed his fifth grade, which was rare at the time in the bush, and spoke acceptable French. This would greatly facilitate our acclimatization. Indeed, Kirundi, the official language of Burundi, is a very complex language built with allusions and proverbs. This makes transmission of information difficult to grasp for a foreigner because the transmission happens between the lines, and the meaning is often hidden and rarely transmitted directly. However, I would learn to discover some of the subtleties of the language during our stay.

First Contact with my Working Universe

It is six o'clock in the morning the day after our arrival and I heard heavy knocks resounding on the door of our lodge. This is the pretty rude military method used by my colleague Robert to get me out of bed without any consideration for Nadine, and to let me know that in half an hour we will attend to the call of workers. During this procedure, we will verify whether the work program is consistent with the established schedule and make necessary adjustments. Half an hour later, we drove the 1.8 miles of track separating our houses from the call center that also marked the beginning of the famous secondary forest of Kibira. During the call, approximately 300 workers were present. This number would grow up to two thousand when the expansion of the plantation and exploitation of the latter would occur simultaneously.

It was my first contact with the extreme poverty of these workers, mostly Hutu, barefoot and wearing patched shorts and tattered loincloths with washed-out colors. The 300 workers were divided into ten teams of 30 men, at the head of which was a supervisor, or *capita*. Workers belonging to the Tutsi ethnic group generally occupied these functions. At that time, the latter usually had a higher level of education than the Hutus and were thus better suited to take positions of responsibility. Further away, as always

---

[15] This term, typical of Belgian colonies, means any employee of the house and has no pejorative or racist connotation.

marginalized and discriminated by Tutsis and Hutus, was a small group of Batwas pygmies who were recruited for their ability to make tools and pottery. As discussed in the following chapters, the Batwas pygmies were also recruited by Hutus to engage in tasks much darker than the manufacture of pottery and tools. It was during the call that I heard for the first time the word *umuzungu* used with the adjective *pili*. *Umuzungu*,[16] used in Rwanda and in Burundi, comes from the Swahili term *mzungu* that meant originally a person who travels frequently from one place to another. By extension, *mzungu* was the name given to white Europeans, while *pili* is the number two and meant that I was the second white in the plantation.

Once the call ended, my colleague and I walked for a few hundred yards on a dirt road sinking into the depths of the forest that stretched out of sight and joined a first group of workers who had received instructions to clear the forest. Then I saw a few acres of deforested land and a small experimental plot of tea established three years before to assess the adaptability of the culture of tea in the climatic conditions of Teza. The technical information collected on this plot along with the climatic information gathered over the same period, were of utmost importance. Indeed, they were required to demonstrate that tea culture was a viable option to diversify high altitude agriculture in Burundi and carry out the work of what would become seven years later the first plantation of about 1,250 acres of industrial tea in Burundi.

From the City to the Bush, From Theory to Practice

Human beings are fascinating because their adaptation skills are quite incredible. Indeed, going from the cozy comfort we were enjoying in town to austere living conditions in the bush was not obvious. Moving from a gas stove to a wooden stove often making cooking rather unpredictable, was in fact not easy. In addition, the cooking time had to be adapted to the altitude since the boiling point of water drops with the decrease in atmospheric pressure. These two factors combined were not conducive to an easy cooking. As to the kerosene refrigerator, its famous capricious and unpredictable wicks make it just as capricious. It had to be

---

[16] Regional variation of the word *mzungu*.

constantly monitored to prevent poor combustion, which would manifest as black smoke followed by a rapid thaw. In terms of water supply, it was not reliable during the rainy season due to the impracticality of the road from the river Nyabigondo to our lodge. In addition, the power supply, limited from 6 p.m. to 10 p.m., proved to be rather unreliable and did not facilitate our life. The old generator dating from before the Second World War was indeed very tired. Breakdowns were frequent. Since Burundi is not far from the equator, day length was almost constant throughout the year with a maximum variation of half an hour. The sun rose around 6 a.m. and set around 6 p.m. Therefore, candlelight or kerosene lantern evenings were numerous. As for the voltage, it should have been 220 volts, but generally ranged between 150 and 200 volts. This constant oscillation did not facilitate the use of some of the electrical appliances we brought along from Belgium. Finally, rainfall was abundant at the beginning of the short rainy season, making our lodge soaking wet despite the fire lit in the early morning by Joseph and that we let die in the early evening. Yet, Nadine the city dweller quickly adapted to these rather peculiar living conditions in a way that has always deeply surprised me.

As for me, I quickly realized that there is a huge difference between university theory and agricultural practice. Deforestation proved an extremely arduous job because prior to undertaking it, a technical and chemical assessment of the forest land that might be converted for tea production ought to be done. To make this assessment, I have crisscrossed tirelessly this secondary ombrophilous forest, also called rainforest, rich in biodiversity and valuable timber. The most notable species include the African Mahogany (*Entandrophragma*), whose lightweight cedar-scented deep reddish brown wood was highly appreciated for cabinetwork and which can reach 200 feet in height and 6.6 feet in trunk diameter; and the African Cherry (*Prunus Africana*), a magnificent tree with perennial green foliage also known for its medicinal properties.[17] I also discovered an astonishing vegetation defying time, as some species such as lichens, arborescent ferns, mosses and epiphytes were real living fossils. Preceded by a few workers who cleared my way with a machete in the dense forest, I had to materialize on the ground units of 9.9 acres that will subsequently be surveyed and mapped. To achieve this objective we progressed, guided by my compass according to north-south axes, cutting

---

[17] Treatment of benign prostatic hypertrophy.

every 656 feet by east-west axes. The same technique will also be used for the latter axes. Like a climber scaling a cliff, I mounted slopes of 60° to 70°[18] to make a preliminary identification of lands unsuitable for tea production due to potential erosion risks and landslides. This is why I eliminated all slopes above 45°, as deemed unsuitable for tea production. These areas were therefore not cleared. This backbreaking work was hardly helped by the rain and cold. Rains were frequent and heavy during the short rainy season, which runs from mid-October to early January. Moreover, their violence doubles during the long rainy season, which lasts from February to May. During those long hours spent in the forest, I came across several families of chimpanzees, baboons, guenons and black colobus monkeys, as well as African servals and civets. I also became acquainted with two species of poisonous snakes: the particularly dangerous Gabon viper (*Bitis gabonica*), one of the longest venomous snakes in the world measuring up to 5.3 feet, and the no less dreadful green viper, or Great Lakes bush viper (*Atheris nitschei*), measuring about 24 inches --hard to spot because it blends easily with the foliage.

Fortunately, workers walking barefoot preceded me and knew how to spot them. The Gabon viper emits its characteristic hissing when approached and the Great Lakes bush viper has a color that differs subtly from the surrounding foliage. A miscalculation and the bite of these individuals can be fatal or lead to amputation of the bitten limb. These workers have taught me how to walk in the forest, the senses always alert. They also showed me that the Gabon viper, feared by many and fierce hunter at dusk, is actually non-aggressive and drowsy during the day. Therefore, I had the chance to attend a unique scene during which a worker stroked the neck of a Gabon viper with his machete. The reptile seemed to appreciate being pet and became calm. Then, the worker grabbed it by the neck with his hands and it showed no particular hostility! This fascinating world marked by constant discoveries and adventures will be mine for seven unforgettable years.

When sufficient clearance was established[19] and slope and soil survey completed, deforestation of the land deemed suitable for tea plantation could start in earnest. When the latter operation had progressed significantly, I started using my optical theodolite to do the land survey and mapping of the land already cleared and

---

[18] A 100% slope is equivalent to 45°.
[19] North-south and east-west axes.

of the forestland that would be kept in its natural state. I did the same with the roads and tracks. Looking back at the topographical work, I realized I still laugh. Indeed, when my manager and I visited Teza for the first time, he told me that one of my responsibilities would include a topographical survey of the entire plantation and the mapping of the latter. He insisted that such a work was of utmost importance to demonstrate to the Government and the European Economic Community funding the tea production program the progress made towards the annual targets agreed upon including deforestation, plantation and road network. Of course, when my manager asked me if I was familiar with topographic work, I replied that I should have no problem since topography was one of the classes taught in the first academic year of the Master's program and that it included practical surveys work. The truth, however, was very different and I knew virtually nothing about topography. Indeed, I attended few of the lectures and labs of this course and my grade during the final exam was only the reflection of my remarkable assiduity and knowledge. Fortunately, topography was only one course among 24! To palliate my severe deficiency in topography, I asked a friend in Belgium to rush me the lectures and lab courses. In this way, I would tend to my theoretical and practical gaps. Whilst theory proved to be relatively easy to master, the use of a theodolite for measuring horizontal and vertical angles proved to be much more complex. Like a true beginner that I was, I started surveying the parking lot in front of my lodge. At first, I used a tape measure to verify the length recorded and see if my calculations were correct and I did the same with the angles using a compass. Fortunately, my colleague, Robert, did not have any clue as to how a theodolite functions and what I was doing in the parking lot. Therefore, I did not have any problem convincing him that I first had to calibrate my instrument in the parking lot before undertaking my survey in the field. Gradually, however, topography would hide no more secrets from me.

A Terrible Tragedy

November 26, 1963, two weeks after our arrival. I returned that morning from the call center to have breakfast. A few minutes later, I saw a white Volkswagen coming driven by Mr. John, the director of ISABU tea production. "I have bad news for you," he said. I expected anything, but not what he was about to say. He told me that my mom had died the day before, on November 25, in a car accident in Guise in northern France. I had the impression of living a bad dream, but it was reality. Here I was, so far away, at the end of the world, isolated on my hill. I would never see her again. I was stunned, shocked by the sudden accidental death. I did not return to Europe due to lack of time since Mom had to be buried two days after the accident. A few days later, however, I received her last letter written a week before her death. She wanted to share with us her happiness to know that Nadine and I had left so confident and full of joy to live our lives in this mysterious Africa. She also mentioned that she would see us as soon as possible. Adventures and travel had always been part of her life and the distant Africa fascinated her. However, this time the beautiful dream was shattered brutally on this narrow road in northern France where a truck crashed into the front of her car. With the shock of the collision, a suitcase located in the back seat broke her neck. That Renault Dauphine was a curse; Nadine and I had a terrible accident in that very same car a year before when the car flipped three times in a turn on a small road in Denmark. Fate is strange, isn't it? The days passed and I needed to read Mom, to see pictures, to live my memories, by myself. I wanted to live my grief alone fully and to the end. Later, when I went to her grave at Guise in France, I planted there a dwarf cedar tree. This tree belongs to the *Cupressaceae* family and is therefore a close relative of the cypress trees that demarcate the Kibira forest, our forest. In this way, I came full circle, in my own way I conveyed to my mom what she never would see. The cedar is now almost 40 years old and reminds me every time I visit my mom's grave that life is so fragile and that we must enjoy every moment of it.

The Inauguration of the Rural Clinic

December 1963. During the month, we received an invitation from the local administration of Busangana (now Bukeye); a small town located 9.3 miles from Teza, asking us to attend the opening of their rural clinic. We were honored and decided to wear the clothes that we thought appropriate for the occasion. The rainy season was well advanced and we arrived at the clinic under a pouring rain. The center was an austere building whose surroundings was poorly drained and extremely muddy and did not facilitate access for visitors in general and for Nadine in particular with the shoes she had put on. A large crowd was waiting for the inauguration and Tutsi dancers commonly called *intore*, literally "the elected," were getting ready to offer a show that was fascinating in every respect.

The administrator greeted us warmly in broken French and introduced us to a group of notables. Then we met Roger, a young Belgian doctor on duty at the hospital in Muramvya, the third largest city in Burundi, distant from Teza by about 15.5 miles. After that, a bewitching ballet began. This ballet represented war dances, solos and group movements. It allowed these slender Tutsi dancers, dressed in leopard or serval skins, ankles taken in rings of bells and wearing white manes, to show their dexterity with the bow and the javelin while highlighting their grace and flexibility of their rhythmic dance. This ballet was supported by music from wind instruments and an orchestra consisting of seven to nine drums that produced an explosion of intricate, hypnotic and exciting rhythms. The drums were of three kinds--there were large drums or *igishikizo*, smaller drums or *ishako,* and finally a drum wearing the colors of Burundi or *inkiranya*.

At the beginning of the ballet, the dancers came in turn in front of the hosts, bowing, straightening the torso and swinging their arms holding a shield or spear. This is the love to greet, the welcoming ritual that initiates all *intore* exhibitions. Next was a succession of battle scenes. The dancers advanced, retreated, moved on one side then on the other. They contorted themselves, ran, bowed down, swelled out their chest and brandished their weapons. Beating at the rhythm of the drums a ground that was trembling and echoed with a more and more intense rumble amplified even more by the bells, with hostile faces, they advanced with their spears pointed forward, stopping abruptly three feet away from us. Awesome! Then, the dancers marked the end of their dance, brandishing their weapons and uttering a long cry.

Intore dancers
(Picture: Courtesy of Michèle De Coninck)

After that, we were treated to a tour of the clinic, unfortunately poor in equipment and drugs. Our disappointment did not escape the head of the clinic who told us that drug supply was deliberately limited for the moment because the staff had to be trained first and had to learn the use and appropriate dose of each drug. He appeared, however, very confident in the future and assured us that the clinic would be fully functional within a few months. The reality would be quite different, as I shall observe throughout my stay in Teza. The shortage of drugs will be commonplace because of poor management and severe lack of funding.

An Ongoing Challenge

The days passed each bringing new landscapes and emotions. I adapted gradually to the working conditions and rigorous lifestyle. Pushing to the west the tail of the December rains, the month of January 1964 marked the beginning of the short dry season that settled for a few weeks. Suspended between heaven and earth, a light veil softened the glare of the sun and gave to colors the opalescence of watercolor. This season allowed a significant advancement in the work of clearing and burning, but also brought its share of accidents. I traveled tirelessly, delimited square blocks of 9.9 acres to facilitate the land survey in this extremely dense forest and calculated the slopes. I used my soil sampler probe to check out soil compaction and detect the presence of layers of stones preventing root penetration. These soils would be unfit for tea plantation. I also did a preliminary analysis of the soil composition and texture by touching or tasting the soil to have an initial idea of its physical structure, clay content, and water-holding capacity, which are important criteria for tea growing. During this process, I learned that farmers have developed a comprehensive knowledge system by which they can understand their soils and the problems in a very particular way. Therefore, I often listened to farmers to better understand their methods of assessing soil fertility, which often can be more precise than the soil testing laboratory results, to refine my own ones. This is how I contributed to the soil surveys and to the decision making process about soil selection for tea growing. During the course of the day, I would crisscross the forest, oversee the development of nurseries, the plantation works, and even to the construction of bridges and roads. Every morning, I also had to measure the stream flow rate of the Nyabigondo River to gather essential flow data to be used for the construction of the turbine that would provide electricity for the future tea factory. One had to know everything and do everything. The work was particularly challenging and difficult when it came to digging the road after making all required surveying in the deep forest, or to build a vehicular timber bridge. Hundreds of workers were affected every day by this rough task. They were digging, terracing and moving the earth with spades and baskets. There was no mechanical support. If the clay content was too high, which could make the road treacherous and even impassable in the rainy season, it was necessary to bring an impressive amount of stones that were subsequently broken and used to build two parallel tire tracks.

Then, in early February began that famous long rainy season, which made working conditions and travel particularly difficult. The dirt roads were particularly dangerous and landslides frequent. In my travels, I used either my Jeep Willis, which was in every way similar to that which had proved itself during the Second World War, or my all-terrain motorcycle. The latter one reminded me of my crazy years when I participated in motorcycle races in Belgium at the end of high school. Sometimes I drove the truck if I felt that the driver, who was a heavy drinker, was too inebriated to drive. By late afternoon, I might also take the tractor equipped with a shovel to prepare in the valley a soccer field for the workers. I had indeed decided to start a soccer team I was part of and organize meetings with local clubs.

The jeep

Clearing

Clearing

Road construction

Road construction

As for the working conditions of workers, they were extremely demanding in terms of physical performance and health, whereas working regulations left little room for tolerance. Undernourished, without rain gear except for some plastic bags, the personnel had to work under any condition except in extreme cases. They had to do strenuous work for tasks such as square yard labor, digging a fixed number of holes to prepare the planting of tea plants, pruning a fixed number of tea plants, and even the digging of roads by the linear yard. In terms of discipline, I had to be strict without going overboard. The 7 a.m. call had to be strictly adhered to, without making any difference between workers living near the plantation or those who had to walk three to four hours to get to the calling point. For the latter workers, the day began at three or four a.m. and ended at nightfall. It was a grueling pace of life for low wages. Generally, workers arriving late could not participate in the labors and therefore would lose the benefit of their meager wages. I do remember clearly that during the frequent heavy rains of the rainy season, the workers, having rags as their only clothes, barefoot, numbed from the cold, would try to find shelter from the elements as best they could. Under these conditions, I had to show empathy while remaining firm and urge the workers to resume work as soon as the rain would subside. From the point of view of health, the working conditions during rainy seasons were, of course, extremely harsh. The frequent rains would prevent clothes from drying and respiratory diseases were unfortunately very common. Overall, the working conditions for the personnel were extremely harsh at Teza when I started working in late 1963. Before all, I was fully accountable for meeting the objective of the tea program and its cost. In doing so, I had to combine firmness and flexibility in carrying out my duties. At the same time, I had to avoid falling in the easy trap of inflexible firmness followed by some of my colleagues or acquaintances. Their behavior towards the workers had not yet melted in the mold of the very recent independence and of the subsequent changes, it would cause in the relationships between expatriates and locals. I was constantly confronted with this difficult duality, but I believe that I managed to maintain strength and flexibility when needed. In retrospect, I think in all objectivity that I was able to create relationships based on respect with the workers and not draw deep enmities against me. The latter case would have had tragic consequences in the severe political turmoil we witnessed during our stay and that I describe later in this book.

These first months were therefore an absorbing experience, sometimes complicated, delicate and costly in efforts. It was a learning period, an investment for the year to come. I had to shake up some preconceived ideas and remain available for surprises–and surprises would come. I experienced that period of tranquility and non-tranquility while fulfilling my professional obligations. What mattered above all was to find the moral strength to go beyond my limits of endurance, to endure physical strains, to face uncomfortable places and to go through severe weather conditions. The humidity and the torrential rains of the rainy season were making tracks and roads slippery and dangerous. I welcomed, however, the cold, low humidity climate of the long dry season stretching from June to September. This season would bring temperatures around 32°F in the lowlands, turning dew into white crystals and bringing a magical hue to the tea plants. My work was an ongoing challenge and I found myself often alone to tackle both technical and human problems. These last ones would leave the deepest impact on me.

The Batwas and the Hunt

When we were in Teza, the Batwas lived mainly from gathering food, making pottery and hunting; the women gather berries, fruits, insects, leaves, mushrooms, nuts, and roots and the men hunt. Batwas are indeed hunters phenomenally gifted. Their small stature undoubtedly enables them to move about the forest more efficiently than taller peoples. Additionally, their smaller body mass allows Pygmies to dissipate their body heat more efficiently. At that time, they did not cultivate the land and maintained close ties with the forest they revered and protected for generations. This was the realm of the Batwas peoples: a forest full of sustenance, shelter and medicine. Many of them have settled in afterwards because the forest has receded and wild animals are endangered. This resulted in a complete loss of the Batwas' traditional economic, social and cultural modes of expression. In the evenings after work Nadine, Johnny and I would often go around the edge of the Kibira forest. What is more beautiful than to contemplate the majestic beauty of this magnificent forest, listening to birdsongs and the cries of monkeys swinging from branch to branch at the sight of Johnny? Often we passed the Batwas who were going hunting or were coming back from it armed with bows and poisoned arrows and spears. Their hunting dog, the *basenji*, sometimes called the Nyam-Nyam Terrier or Congo Terrier, accompanied them. The *basenji* is a primitive dog that does not bark, but it can make sounds that resemble the howling, grunting and even the Tyrolean song. As for the Batwas' bow, it is generally made of a reinforced bamboo split down in the middle. The arrows used are different depending on the game hunted. The iron-tipped bamboo or hardened coated poison is for hunting monkeys, while wooden arrows are used for hunting birds. As for reptiles, they are not hunted by the Batwas and are forbidden as food. The spirits of the forest are believed to inhabit within reptiles, which are therefore considered as animal protectors. What a fascinating sight to see these small men go hunting with their dogs using weapons that have changed little for thousands of years and return laden with rodents, primates and birds. The Batwas trade a portion of their bush meat for manioc, produce, and other goods whilst they preserve the rest for their own consumption using drying, salting, or smoking conservative practices.

A Freak Accident

At noon, I used to come back home for lunch. One day around 1 p.m., I was informed that a severe accident occurred when clearing the fields. I drove my jeep, left it down a hill where the clearing was in progress, and then walked the one and a half mile separating me from the site of the accident. When I arrived on the spot, the shock was terrible and words cannot express what I saw, heard and felt. I was petrified. About fifty men were indeed buried in a hole under an enormous stump measuring more than 20 feet in diameter and weighing a few tons. Fatality and clearing practices caused this carnage. Indeed, when clearing a large stump, workers generally go into the hole of an old stump, here about 100 feet from the stump in question. This hole serves as a support to pull a stump with steel cables and a hand winch. Normally when the stump begins to move, workers quickly evacuate their position. In this case, the stump lashed at once from its base, quickly gained momentum due to its weight and buried within seconds the unfortunate who did not have time to flee. There were many dead and severely wounded with legs either amputated or completely dislocated. The ground was red with the blood, which kept flowing while moaning covered the noise of the surviving workers who were trying to reach their comrades. The wounded need to be cleared as soon as possible but how can several tons of stump be moved? We also had to quickly stop the external bleeding; we had to stop the flow of red blood with which life was leaving on that hill of death. I was alone in making decisions, alone with this heartbreaking scene. I called for additional workers to move the stump with cables and hand winches. A time that seemed endless passed before it moved and ran down the hill freeing the dead and the wounded ones. The workers and I grasped lianas and made improvised tourniquets. Then we had to separate the dead from the wounded and carry these last ones up the road. The less severely affected were transported on the back of others while the most serious wounded men were carried on improvised stretchers.

I brought the tractor and trailer and we placed the wounded next to each other. I took care of the more severely wounded and had them placed in my jeep. Then the convoy headed to the nearest hospital in Muramvya managed by our friend Roger, a doctor. The journey was endless: half an hour with the jeep and about an hour with the tractor. When we arrived at the hospital, the nurse on duty looked at us haggard and nearly fainted at the sight of these mutilated bodies, and then he rushed inside the hospital hallooing for nurses. As for me, I went looking for Roger, who lived a mile from the hospital. In the latter, there was no room left and the wounded were lying down on the floor in the corridors. All night Roger operated or rather amputated to address the most critical situations. The tractor and I made an additional trip to transport the dead to the morgue at Muramvya. This day marked me forever and the stigma are still so fresh in my memory. When I think back about that fateful event, when I think back about that hell, about those unfortunates whose lives were shattered forever, I relive this nightmare and I still shudder.

The Family Grows

April 21, 1964. Mid-April 1964, I drove Nadine to some friends in Bujumbura so that she would be near the Prince Rwagasore Clinic where she was scheduled to give birth soon. Indeed, staying in the bush in the rainy season and waiting until the last moment was too risky because landslides were frequent and would often cut the road off for a while. Then, I went back to Teza and waited until I was informed of the imminence of this happy event. On April 20, at 7:30 a.m., I was told by phone that the birth would be triggered the next day. I jumped into my VW and immediately drove down, but found myself stuck mid-way by a huge mudslide cutting the road and extending over a length of approximately 330 feet. What was I supposed to do? I did not have any other alternative but to try to drive through mud bed. Indeed, to make a huge detour to another dirt road would have been highly speculative and expecting the arrival of a bulldozer to clear the road was a pious dream. So I ventured out on foot to measure the depth of the mud and then I decided to go for broke. I picked up speed and went through, or rather slipped due to the flat bottom of the car, this layer of mud as a skier on the snow. I finally arrived at the clinic in time to witness the birth of our son, Eric on April 21 at 8:30 a.m. When our son was born, we had a delicious moment of love, tenderness and intimacy. We were so happy. Outside, the flowers of the flamboyant trees glistened with orange glares as if nature wanted us to celebrate the birth by gratifying us with its most beautiful colors. Shortly after the delivery, I went to the post office to send a telegram in Belgium to announce the happy event. A few days later, we went back into our bush where Eric grew up until he was six years old.

Rwagasore Clinic

Telegram

Of course, life in the bush in our house with a newborn, a power supply nonexistent during the day and most capricious in the evening, and a kerosene lamp as the only source of dim light at night was not simple. The nights were cold and wet and our room, or rather our cellar, was just the same. Eric, for reasons of course unknown to us was crying every night. We could not make him stop. Yet someone managed to calm him down and make him sleep without us requesting anything from this person. Our *zamu*, a common name for a guard or sentry, an almost six and a half foot tall Tutsi would break into our house when he heard wailing and begin to sing and clap. This caused Eric to fall asleep quickly every time! Then our *zamu* would go back in front of his fire, and continue singing until late at night while drinking warm beer for which he had a strong inclination. We loved our *zamu* dearly!

Visits of the Mwami

In 1964 and 1965, during the short and long dry seasons we had the honor and pleasure to receive in our very modest cottage on multiple occasions the King of Burundi, Mwami Mwambutsa IV. His chauffeur would drive him to Teza in his white convertible Cadillac accompanied by his bodyguard and his mistress, as white as his Cadillac. January 1964 was the first time we met with the King. He immediately put us at ease poking fun at Nadine's growing belly and expressing interest in what she was doing to occupy herself in the bush. We discovered that the King was fond of strawberries, very abundant in front of our lodge, but that he was a true lover of whiskey. During these many visits that we came to know the King of Burundi very well. The King was very simple man of great distinction who was always pleased to come to our small cottage and drink a few glasses of whiskey while workers were picking strawberries and his mistress and bodyguard were waiting for him in this immaculate Cadillac. We enjoyed this awesome show and memorable visits of this great man.

The Bushmen Go Into Town

Isolated on our hill we needed to recharge our batteries on a regular basis, to make contact again with civilization, to see the world, to go to the restaurant, and to savor the joys of the beach or pool. We therefore decided to go down to Bujumbura on Sundays as often as possible to spend the day. We made the journey in our 1956 American Ford that I brought from Belgium soon after our arrival in Burundi. This choice was a little crazy, but it sometimes takes a touch of madness in life, because this vehicle was not particularly suited to the small tracks leading to the plantation or to the road conditions that were especially difficult in the rainy season. Our dog always came with us and he shared the backseat with Eric who was traveling in his very rustic straw bed. Indeed, we, the bushmen had no sophisticated transportation for Eric who therefore never experienced the joys and comfort of the stroller! We usually went to the club of the Entente Sportive to enjoy the pool and drove into this impressive azure blue car, which did not pass unnoticed with a child in a strange straw cradle and an imposing dog. No one knew us and we knew no one. Later, when we had the opportunity to meet some people, the tongues untied and we really enjoyed hearing what the citizens of Bujumbura thought of us. Indeed, this very special community going to the pool and comprising of mostly foreigners often had not much to talk about except gossips, and especially those on the lives of others. We were told that many people wondered where this strange couple did come from, traveling in an unusual car, with a large dog not particularly well-educated, and who could not afford a stroller like everyone else but used a straw bed like Africans! I also heard that the father seemed a little bit flaky and irresponsible, as he would throw his few-months-old son in the deep end of the pool while he could not walk yet and had to fend for himself to regain the edge. Later, his sister also underwent the same training to learn to swim and the results turned out to be excellent! Finally, this odd couple having lunch on the terrace of the club with this wretched straw bed on a chair and this rather badly educated dog begging at the table, went off as it had come to an unknown destination! This is what Bujumbura was, with its gossips and hearsays!

Entente Sportive

Eric in his straw cradle

Our Ford

Our Ford

Our Move

After 18 months in our lodge, the houses built on the plantation were finally ready to welcome us. What a contrast to our lodge. Finally, we had a living room, two bedrooms and a bathroom relatively well fed with hot and cold water coming from a large gas drum recycled in a tank connected to the plumbing until the water tower was built. African plumbing may be rudimentary, but it is effective. As in our lodge, the tank was regularly filled with water that needed to be carried from the river. Finally, we had a new generator that worked most of the day and delivered a stable voltage. The gestation of this house was long but the pleasure of living in it and in the bush with a modern twist was only bigger.

Our house

The water supply

The Ambush

Every month, Nadine and I were driving down to Bujumbura to make our supplies and take money from the bank to pay the workers. I would drive down with a metallic trunk box because the volume of notes was significant since I needed small change. The total amount I collected from the bank was of course important since we had 2,000 regular workers on the payroll. After completing most of our shopping, I would collect the money early in the afternoon and place the metallic box in the trunk of the car. Then we would make our last purchases of perishables. In the evening, we usually went to the restaurant before going back up in the bush long after night had fallen. Often, we would meet near Bugarama, layers of fog so dense that visibility was reduced to a few meters and in such cases, the only reference point was the centerline of the road. The risk of accidents was high because I had to follow that central line for several miles. Fortunately, the presence of vehicles at these late hours was rare. Aside from the danger caused by the fog, it never occurred to me or to my employers that going back into the bush at night with a considerable amount of money was a risky operation. In fact, we could easily be the target of attacks by armed gangs. Indeed, all the staff and workers of the plantation were of course aware of the purpose of these monthly visits to the city and it would have been easy for some of them to mount an attack. Everything went normal for 20 months and then one night it was nearly drama. It was about midnight when, after leaving the main road, we took the small tortuous access road leading to the plantation. I was driving slowly because the track, flooded by a downpour, was very slippery. Suddenly, at the exit of a turn one whose image is enshrined forever in my memory, I noticed in front of my headlights two tree trunks across the road. It was clear that I was expected and I did not have to wait a long time as I suddenly saw, a few dozen yards away from the vehicle, a handful of men armed with machetes preparing to descend the slope overlooking the road. Things were getting tough, but luck was on my side. Indeed, the place to block a vehicle was badly chosen because the turn was relatively wide and eventually allowed time to turn around. Everything was played in a few seconds. I drove to my left toward the slope, which surprised the attackers obviously, then I abruptly stopped the vehicle, and finally I did a quick reverse and left in the other direction. We had a narrow escape and I hate to think of what would have happened to us if the ambush had been successful. I took the main road and after a few miles, I went on a forest path, which we followed for about 10 miles through a eucalyptus afforesting, before joining the other side of the plantation. Then, I headed to my office to place money in the safe. This attempted embezzlement should have alerted my direction on the potential dangers posed by the transportation of funds at night, unarmed. Such was not the case as it was supposedly difficult to obtain a permit to carry a weapon. As for granting me a specific day to get the money and come back during the day, it was out of the question. In retrospect, my conclusion is clear. The potential risks incurred by expatriates living in the bush are of little concern to those living in Bujumbura. I received confirmation later about this rigid narrow-mindedness of my management during other events taking place in Teza. It was obvious that the work took precedence over all other considerations because the compliance objectives of the investors of the tea project were essential.

The Wedding of My Burundian Friend

July 1965. During my studies at the Faculty of Gembloux, I had befriended a Burundian student who started his studies two years after me. The son of a wealthy family whose father had held several ministerial posts, my friend Alexis graduated in June 1965 and returned home to marry. I was greatly surprised when he asked Nadine to be the maid of honor at his wedding. The preparations were grandiose and Nadine was wearing *Imvutano*, the traditional multi-colored Burundian dress for ceremonies. The wedding ceremony took place in the groom's house located on a hill overlooking Bujumbura. We had the privilege and the opportunity to intensely enjoy the traditions of this wedding ceremony where food and drinks are a major activity. Meals included fish; goat and hen livened up with plantains, beans and tubers such as cassava, yams, taro, potato and sweet potatoes. We also shared the calabash gourd containing this delicious banana beer we were drinking with a long sorghum straw. The ceremony was adorned by an unforgettable performance of *intore* dancers wearing leopard-skin, celebrating their warriors' achievements with their dances mimicking the battles they had won. The performance would not be complete without the colorful participation of drummers or the tales of legends and tributes and pirouettes following one another on the spur of each.

Nadine, maid of honor

In the Land of Joys and Sorrows

Nadine and the future wedded man

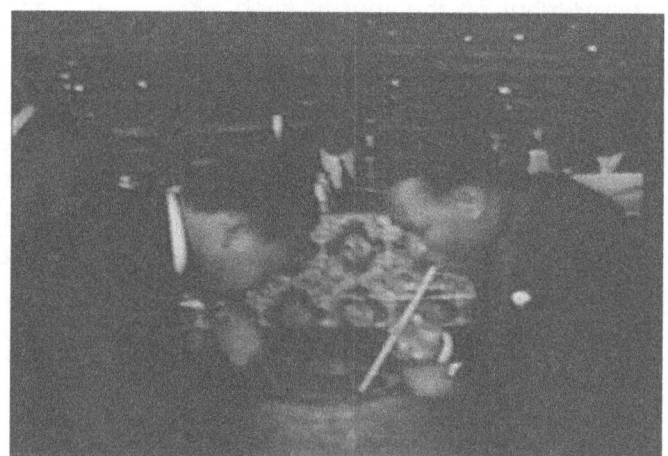
The calabash

Nadine

The Dreadful Carbon Monoxide

August 1965. One morning while I was driving to one of the points of call, I saw a crowd of a dozen employees in front of the house of my agronomist, located on the other side of the factory. I stopped my car to hear them say that my agronomist, Deo, was discovered inert in his room. I entered into this little house, headed for the bedroom and found Deo lying dead on his bed. Not far from it was a wood burner with a few embers still burning. Obviously, my poor Deo died poisoned by carbon monoxide produced by his stove in this enclosed space as all windows were closed. We were in the dry season, the temperature was often reaching 32 °F during the night and use of wood fires was common in both houses and in the huts.

Two employees raised the body to take it in my car, a VW Beetle, to drive him to the hospital in Muramvya to record his death. However, we quickly realized that it was totally impossible to fit this body of nearly 6.5 feet in my car because it had stiffened and we could not bend his legs. Truck and tractor were already gone to work and I had no alternative but to try to squeeze the body of my poor agronomist in my car. We tried, but to no avail. There was one macabre option left: put the body in the rear of the car and leave his legs hanging out the open window. I then shut the window up half way trapping the legs. This is how I made this funeral and incredible trip of about 15 miles separating Teza from the hospital, Muramvya.

Religious Festivals

I also had the opportunity to meet religious leaders and obtained their agreement to attend two very important and beautiful religious festivals that were part of the traditional culture of Burundi. The first one, *kubandwa*, celebrates the harvest of grain and pays tribute to Kiranga, a spirit which is that of all the dead ancestors. During the ceremony based on the possession of the mind and animated by body expressions, young men paint their bodies, dance and sing traditional songs. One of these men represents Kiranga. At the end of the ceremony, all participants follow a specific ritual and undergo a water-purification in a river.[20] The second ceremony, *umuganuro* or *sorghum*, is the ceremony accompanying the fertility festival. It is accompanied by the beating of drums and dancing and a seedling of sorghum is planted to ensure a good harvest. The First Republic unfortunately abolished this beautiful ceremony organized at the time of the Kingship in 1966 because it wanted to break the royal rhythm and advocate its own values.

---

[20] The film *Le rite du Kubandwa dévoilé* [Kubandwa Rite Unveiled] is of historical and cultural significance. It was produced in 2010 through the collaboration of Ambassadors Fund for the Preservation of Culture managed by the U.S. Embassies Abroad and supported by the Office of the Education and Cultural Affairs at the State Department of Nduwamahoro (People of Peace), the Cultural Expert of the Documentary Father, Adrien Ntabona, and its Director, Léonce Ngabo. This documentary is a major step in preserving the rite and ritual of the Kubandwa cult, once viewed as a major cultural force, not only in Burundi but also in the Great Lakes Region.

V. A LONG ESCAPADE

Our Trip to East Africa

According to my contract, we were entitled to a paid return in Europe every two years and in November 1965, we could have benefited from this long-awaited vacation. However, we decided to wait until spring 1966 to return to Europe and use our local leave to make our first major trip to East Africa. However, we had to wait until Eric decided to walk. Indeed, at 16 months old, Eric was still a very proficient crawler showing no imminent signs of straightening up to the despair of his parents. On the other hand, it had already been several months since he swam comfortably but his talents as a swimmer were unfortunately of no use for our trip. Then, the miracle came. A friend lent us a trotter and a week later Eric was walking! With no further delays, we finalized our travel plans, which included going through Rwanda, Uganda, Kenya, and Tanzania with visits to several national parks. We planned to make a journey of over 3,750 miles in twenty days with our Opel station wagon that was no longer very young since she had reached the 62,000-mile mark.

The ride

September 1965. With the travel plans established, we finalized the administrative preparations, which necessitated no less than four visas—such a task was far from a sinecure for the bushmen we were. Indeed, since we were only allowed two monthly supplies in Bujumbura, we had to make three additional round trips, taken from our holidays to meet all administrative and medical formalities. After five weeks, we had all the necessary visas and vaccinations. We then prepared our equipment, which we limited to a few spare parts for the car, two gasoline jerry cans because gas would be difficult to find as soon as we departed from the main areas--which we intended to do. We also took a few oilcans, an additional spare wheel because there were many punctures in the bush and in particular on the slopes covered with extremely sharp and abrasive laterite and the everlasting shovel, essential in the bush. We added up a medical kit and few water bottles. In mid-September, we took the direction of Rwanda, the "Land of a Thousand Hills."

As we were still in the dry season, a thick layer of dust accompanied us. It was everywhere, covering the road, giving the leaves and branches of trees along the road colors ranging from yellow to red ocher. This dust entered through the back door of our vehicle and we breathed it continually. Without incident, we crossed the border at Kanyaru, the river separating Rwanda and Burundi, and then took the direction of Butare, Rwanda's second city, which we reached after about an hour of driving. We met a couple of friends who would accompany us with their own vehicle in our journey. Then we planned to make our first stop at the Akagera National Park about 220 miles away from Teza.

Akagera Park

The park covers about 13,500 square miles in eastern Rwanda along the Tanzanian border. A magnificent spectacle awaited us. The park is interspersed with a maze of swamps, lakes, savannah and forests that are home to many wild animals, including monkeys, buffalo, zebras, elephants, rhinos, antelopes and lions. Additionally, along its lakes, it contains one of the largest concentrations of birds on the continent. We spent a full day and night in the park and then headed towards Kagitumba, the border post between Rwanda and Uganda.

Akagera Park

Initial Contact with Uganda

At the border, the immigration and customs formalities took over two hours. Finally, we entered into Uganda where we had to get used to driving on the left, a legacy of British colonization. Soon, this change was largely offset by driving on paved roads. What a miracle after making several hundred miles on bumpy and dusty roads! We then headed to Kampala, Uganda's capital, a distance of 174 miles from the border post. Halfway through, before crossing the equator shortly before Entebbe, the car of our friends unfortunately broke down. With a heavy heart, they were forced to turn back and be towed by a truck to Kigali. Therefore, we continued our journey alone towards Kampala where we stayed overnight before heading to the Murchison Falls National Park.

At the Equator

Murchison Falls National Park

After leaving Kampala, we reconnected with the bumpy roads for a day before entering the national park. This park, cut by the Nile River, which is the longest in the world[21], is named after the impressive Murchison Falls on the Nile falling from 141 feet through an opening of 23 feet. With a superficies of 1,480 square miles, it is the largest in Uganda. In this park we saw an impressive number of hippos, some close to one another on the banks of the river, others clinging together in the water. The most incredible show was to see these several-tons behemoth animals diving into the water from a height of nine to twelve feet while avoiding falling on the back of one of their own, which was far from being obvious. We also observed the Nile monitors (*Varanus niloticus*), the largest

---

[21] The measures vary between 4,038 and 4,163 miles.

lizard in Africa growing up to 7 feet long, musing on the banks of the river, the elephants coming to drink or taking a bath, and finally, one of the largest living saurian in the world after the Australian saltwater crocodile (*Crocodylus porosus*): the Nile crocodile (*Crocodylus niloticus*). The lodge where we spent the night offered us a big surprise. Indeed, while we were on the veranda gazing at this magical landscape, we were greeted by a huge elephant that approached us stopping only a few yards from our table before going to empty a bin, which was not far from there. By visiting the savannah of the park on the way back towards Kenya and Kampala, we also came close to many gazelles, giraffes, lions and a few impressive numbers of buffaloes. The latter posed a serious problem for the ecosystem because the pastures were overgrazed and, therefore, became progressively highly degraded. Visiting this park home to a rich array of spectacular animals will leave us a memorable souvenir.

Hippopotamuses

In the Land of Joys and Sorrows

Eric and hippopotamuses

Mid-day slump

The dive

En route to Kenya and Tanzania

After returning to Kampala, we headed to Kenya and the Masai Mara Reserve. Along the way, we made our first stop at Lake Nakuru, which offered us a unique natural spectacle of some two million flamingos who live there. Then we undertook the long trek on dusty and rutted roads through the Great Rift Valley of East Africa to the Masai Mara national reserve, which we reached in the early evening after a seven-hour drive. This valley is also called the "cradle of humanity" because many hominid fossils and very ancient archaeological remains were discovered there. After an overnight stand in a camp, we hit the road again. We soon met the Masai communities and their herds of cattle, goats and sheep, and the donkeys they use for transportation. The Masai are a Nilotic people who probably migrated from southern Sudan in the 15th century. The whole family is engaged in pastoral farming, the young ones are in charge of animal grazing, the women deal with the milking, and the men are responsible for the enkang[22] fence and general herd management. The number of gates for each enkang represents the number of families living there. The Masai live in houses that look like igloos made of grass and branches assembled with cow dung. The animals live together in the center of the enkang. It is through the contact with the Masai that we

---

[22] Group of houses in a circle, surrounded by a fence made of thorny branches. A set of *enkangs* forms a village called *boma*.

came to appreciate that people can live in perfect harmony and in peace with wild animals. There is also a beautiful Masai proverb, which says that the day belongs to men and the night to wild animals. The time of our visit, towards the end of September, coincided with the great migration of wildebeests and zebras. What a marvel to witness in this reserve belonging to the Masai people the migration of these herbivores and also to observe large Topi antelopes (the largest antelope in the world), small antelopes such as the Thomson's gazelle, slender and elegant, and the Grant's gazelle, with its limpid gaze and exceptional beauty, giraffes, buffalos near marshes and other species that offer a choice of abundant food for large predators such as cheetahs, lions and leopards. Then, we stopped for a while at the Mara River in which hippos were basking, while on the banks the crocodiles, with wide-open fearsome jaws and totally immobile, seemed harmless at first sight. However, crocodiles are fierce predators. Adults can potentially take a wide range of large vertebrates, including antelope, buffalo, young hippos, and large cats. They also have a reputation as man killers.

From Masai Mara to Kilimanjaro

The next day we resumed our road to Moshi in northern Tanzania and reached it after about 200 miles and a full day's drive. Then, we continued our journey towards the area that will become the Kilimanjaro National Park[23]. We spent two nights at the foot of the volcano that is part of a set of three extinct volcanoes (Shira, Mawenzi, and Kibo). With a peak of 19,327 feet[24], Kibo is one of the "kings of Africa." *The Snows of Kilimanjaro*, one of the most mystical writings of Ernest Hemingway, poignantly describes the ascent of this attractive and emblematic mountain. A film of the same name, starring Gregory Peck and Ava Gardner, has also been taken from this dazzling novel. The next day we admired the ice cap summit confined to Kibo. Unfortunately, this ice cap is now in regression partly because of the global warming and mainly, I think, because of human pressure--the human influence exerted on nature and the intense deforestation associated with it, which alters the cycle of water and causes a decrease in precipitation. I also remember, when I returned to Tanzania in 1977, notably in

---

[23] The Kilimanjaro National Park was created in 1973.
[24] Made in 2008 by GPS and gravimetry.

Moshi and Arusha as part of a mission of rural development, having extensively discussed the problem of the decline of the water table with farmers. I noticed in the area that some wells of water supply were completely dry while the water table of other wells had decreased by 65 to 100 feet in 20 to 30 years.

The Kilimanjaro and its eternal snows

Eric the Explorer

The cottage we stayed in at the foot of Kilimanjaro was at an altitude of about 4,000 feet and was located near a savannah formed by many large grass species often exceeding 10 feet mixed with acacia and a few baobabs. Under ideal conditions, going up to the summit of Kilimanjaro and coming back takes about 6 to 10 days for normal hikers. Given our travel schedule, this was of course excluded, especially with Eric who barely walked. Instead of that, we roamed for a day in the savannah admiring the snow-covered tops of the volcano and numerous birds. We also had the chance to enjoy the traditional Chagga[25] huts. These huts have no walls and their roof, made of wooden poles, branches and thorny thatch rests directly on the ground.

The morning of our hike, we took our breakfast on the terrace of our lodge. Eric was sitting quietly with us and then suddenly we

---

[25] The Chagga people, of Chagga language, occupy the southern and eastern slopes of Mount Kilimanjaro, while the Masai occupy the northern and western foothills of the mountain.

lost sight of him. We called him repeatedly but in vain. We tried to look around us but our field of vision was limited by the extremely dense savannah. Panic quickly came. We called the staff of the lodge and a huge search party was organized. Tension rose, time passed and still no sign of Eric. We were not talking anymore. Was he lost? Had there been an accident? Had he been kidnapped? The time factor became important, as a young child is naturally more vulnerable in the bush. Then, after an hour that felt like an eternity, we were reassured. Not far from the terrace of our lodge, we discovered, completely by chance, Eric sitting near an acacia, quietly busy turning the pedals of a bicycle that a staff member of the house had left there, and of course without any concerns for the fear and the emotion that he had caused. Our visit to Kilimanjaro will forever remain associated with the escapade of Eric. In his way, he had explored the foothills of the iconic volcano.

From Kilimanjaro to Nairobi

After our two days of eventful visits, we headed towards Nairobi, Kenya via Moshi, Arusha, Mamanga, which is today the border city between Tanzania and Kenya. In the early evening after about eight hours of drive, we arrived in Nairobi where we intended to spend two to three days before making our way back to Burundi. Since we were used to our bush and to Bujumbura, a modest-sized city, Nairobi was a revelation. With its numerous hotels, department stores, its wide streets and heavy traffic, Nairobi brought us back into the atmosphere of a real city, an atmosphere we had abandoned two years before when leaving Brussels. Therefore, we indulged ourselves during these two days without worrying about money spent. Indeed, I was planning to go to the bank before leaving to cash money to pay our hotel bill and ensure our return. The morning we left, I went to the bank with my checkbook but was told it would take at least five to seven business days to get the money I wanted. Indeed, at that time, the banking system was very backward and banking facilities were quasi non-existent. I was told that I had to first send a telex, the only rapid communication method at that time, to my Bank in Brussels and request them to transfer funds to the Bank of Nairobi. We were stranded in Nairobi with very little money left. In the hotel, we did not have any problem extending our stay because we could prove we were waiting for money. However, for all other expenditures, we were in deep trouble. While waiting for the money transfer, we were obliged to eat as cheap as possible with the exception of Eric who had to have a more balanced diet. We were tempted by so many things that we were deprived from during the last two years, but could not afford anything extra. Every day I went to the bank hopeful, but without success. Finally, on the sixth day the good news came, the money was finally available. We celebrated this happy surprise by going that same night to the best nightclub in Nairobi, which was also considered at the time as one of the bests in Africa. Everything was covered with zebra skin, which fascinated us at the time. After the famine of nearly a week, we spared no expense and the highlight of our evening was the appearance of the famous South African singer, Miriam Makeba, the empress of African song and a symbol of freethinking and tolerance. Her remarkable song *Malaika*, which means angel in Swahili, still resonates in our heart as if it was yesterday.

The Long Way Home

The day after this memorable evening, we headed back towards Uganda and the border of Rwanda. We were driving without problems when suddenly a few miles away from the Rwandan border, the gearbox began to whistle abnormally and then froze in second gear. Obviously, it ran out of oil. We crossed the border and the noise intensified. At any moment, I expected the gearbox to break. In such a case, our only resort would be to wait for a providential truck to pull us to Burundi because the chance of finding a used box would be rather slim. However, we continued our journey without changing speed for about 60 miles, which seemed interminable, before finding a small garage. The mechanic put the car on the pit for a diagnosis. There was no oil in the box but to my surprise, the box seemed intact. After filling it up, we were able to continue our way back. The gearbox seemed new despite the difficult times that the gears had to endure. On October 10, 1965 after 20 days of a memorable trip and more than 4,000 miles, we arrived at the border of Burundi. Three hours later we were back home in Teza. We reunited with our dog, kept by friends, and resumed a more moderate pace of life. Yet, the events that smiled at us during this unforgettable journey shifted suddenly and completely unexpectedly a week after our return.

In the Land of Joys and Sorrows

VI. THE OCTOBER 1965 COUP

The Beginnings of the Coup

May 1965. During this month, the first elections after independence were held. There were no surprises in that the Hutus, by far the majority, won a landslide victory of 23 parliamentary seats out of the 33 available. However, in September 1965, the Mwami decided to appoint one of his Tutsi friends, M. Biha, as Prime Minister in place of a Hutu minister. The Hutus, furious at the decision of Mwami, launched a coup on the night of October 18, 1965. The coup was carried out by a fraction of the Hutu army, the gendarmerie officers and civilians. It began in Bujumbura and expanded according to a predetermined strategy in the province of Muramvya and especially in our location, Teza.

The Coup in Bujumbura

October 18, 1965. During the night a group of Hutu rebels, commanded by the Secretary of State Police Antoine Serukwavu, seized the royal palace and attempted to assassinate the Mwami. Due to an error of the rebels who fought each other, the Mwami was able to leave the palace by the back door and thus saved his life. The mutineers then headed to the residence of Mr. Biha, the Prime Minister. He was riddled with bullets and left for dead in his garden. The next day he was found dying. He was taken to hospital, Rwagasore, then to Europe where he was miraculously saved. The mutineers then went to the barracks near the Royal Athenaeum to seize munitions. Meanwhile, the loyalist troops were organized both in Bujumbura by Captain and future President, Michel Micombero and in Gitega by Commander Paul Rusiga. The latter led his troops to Bujumbura where he arrived at dawn on October 19. Around 10 a.m., the mutiny ended in Bujumbura and most of the mutineers were killed.

The Massacre of Tutsis in Teza

October 19, 1965. As for the previous day, the weather seemed to be rainy and I was happy about it because such conditions favor the planting of tea seedlings. Indeed, the short rainy season had started with some delays and this was affecting the preparations required for tea planting. It was therefore necessary to intensify our efforts and recruit additional labor to achieve our goal of about 250 acres planted during the year. We had about 1,800 workers available and my estimations showed the need to engage at least 300 additional workers by the end of October to achieve our objective. I, therefore, planned to announce at the call of workers that recruitment intensive efforts would be made immediately and that likely candidates would be engaged the next morning. However, the next day and the following days showed, unfortunately, that any strategy, any life could be swept as a wisp of straw by the fury of a human. I got up as usual at dawn, at 6 a.m., and took a quick shower, but not very hot since the wood used to heat our water tank was wet. In addition, as often was the case in the rainy season, the smoke from the fireplace was blowing back and the bathroom was very quickly filled with smoke. Very motivating to get out quickly! Then, I took my jeep and after a quick detour to my office located below the house, I headed towards the Nyamenda hill located about 2.5 miles away. This hill was one of the three call points for plantation workers where approximately 700 workers were there divided into 20 teams. The call began at 7 a.m. and was proceeding normally. I made the recruitment process announcement and twenty minutes later, the workers left for their respective working point by foot or on a tractor, whereas I headed back to my office.

The Coup

Office in the front and the three houses

Before going to my office, I looked at the hillside recently planted with Araucaria, a magnificent evergreen coniferous tree imported from Brazil. No noise, everything was quiet. Then my attention was suddenly drawn to an unusual movement at the bottom of the hill still embedded in the morning fog. Intrigued, I looked more carefully and quickly I was able to distinguish a column composed of about 100 men dressed in white. They were moving silently towards the factory and my office. I remember thinking that it was so strange to find such an important column of men going towards the factory. I also remembered being dazzled by the unusual color of the clothes. I was motionless, stunned and thoughtful for about five minutes. Then I saw Nestor, my storekeeper. He was heading towards the column of men. Moreover, these men were armed with machetes, spears, clubs and sharp-pointed iron pieces. Within this column consisting essentially of Hutus, I also saw some Pygmies. To see them amongst a group of Hutus was, however, bizarre. Indeed, Pygmies who worked in the plantation were all assigned tasks manufacturing tools, tasks they mastered remarkably, but never mixed with the two other ethnic groups who disdained them. It would only be later that morning that I came to understand their presence and role.

I hailed my storekeeper and asked him what he was doing at the head of these men. "You'll see," was his reply. "See what?" I asked him. "Since you insist, I am informing you that last night there was a coup against the Tutsi government and against the

Mwami in Bujumbura. My uncle, who was head of the coup, asked me to ensure the coup will spread inside the country. My men and I will, therefore, launch a full fledge attack to eliminate all your Tutsi personnel living in the compound on the other side of the factory[26], and then we will kill your Tutsi agronomist who lives next to you." I could not believe that such human barbarity would materialize and that men would be killing other men cold-blooded like wild beasts. I stood dumbfounded and shocked. Then, powerless in front of such a column of men in a state of excitement, I decided to return to my office and establish as every morning at 7:30 a.m. the radio contact with the management of ISABU in Bujumbura. I sat down, turned the radio dial and was about to start the usual signal "hello Bujumbura, hello Bujumbura, this is Nyabigondo calling." At that point, Nestor came to my office and told me calmly and politely, "Boss, if you do not turn off the radio immediately, I'll have to kill you!" For the first time in my life I saw death in front of me and she said "turn the radio off before it's too late," and so, this is what I did. I was in a daze, but oddly enough, I never felt fear at the sight of the men in this column, or during the death threat issued by Nestor or even during the terrible times that followed. However, I decided to try to leave the plantation with my family because I thought that this ethnic cleansing under preparation could well escalate and that our lives might be threatened. Indeed, recent events in the neighboring Congo including rapes, lootings and massacres of the whites were very frequent and were illustrating the potential danger of being isolated and white in this barbaric insurgency. As Nestor was responsible for the fuel depot, I asked him to give me a jerry can of about 5 gallons of fuel, as the tank of my car was nearly empty. He immediately understood that I wanted to leave the plantation and told me that I would have to stay here until the end of the coup to ensure that I would alert neither my management nor the authorities. He further told me that in order to prevent any escape or army counter-attack they had cut the three bridges giving road access to the hill where the factory and houses were located. We were stranded.

I kept my cool and nevertheless ordered him to bring me the jerry can I had requested. Remaining very respectful towards me, he coldly replied that he would bring it to me when he and his men passed through our garden to kill my fellow Tutsi agronomist. What a sinister response! I was living a nightmare! I came home

---

[26] This staff included secretaries, typists and agricultural technicians.

The Coup

and explained to Nadine that there were some serious troubles in the plantation without going into specific details. Yet it was impossible to hide the truth any longer when inhuman tears, groans and cries started to be heard. The savage massacre of the Tutsis had begun in the camp. It lasted nearly an hour and then the noise faded before stopping completely.

We did not know what to do and escaping seemed impossible. We had to wait, wait, and perhaps wait for death. In addition, we had no weapons to defend ourselves except my underwater spear gun powered by compressed air. Of course, this gun, which throws a spear with a sharp tip, is capable of piercing a man, but it is a worthless weapon when facing a hundred men armed with spears and machetes. The minutes went on, yet neither Nadine nor I apparently lost our composure. Were we afraid or not? I had no answer since the events that had just started, and of which we still did not suspect the amplitude, appeared to us so unreal.

Then, suddenly, the noise started again. I looked through the glass door of our house and saw the column of men led by my storekeeper, singing in a state of extreme excitation, heading towards the entrance to our garage. Curiously, at the head of this column were threatening Pygmies brandishing their bows, arrows and machetes. They seemed bewitched. I learned later that they were drugged with hemp. At this point, I thought all was lost, we would die, die a violent death on that distant hill lost in the forest. Above all, I thought about my family, about Nadine who had followed me to the end of the world and had left everything and about Eric who was just beginning to discover the world. I felt guilty. Then, my life that seemed so short flashed before my eyes, with its good and less good times. Was it going to end abruptly on this lost hill in the secondary forest? Were we going to suffer the fate that too many Europeans have experienced during the independence of the neighboring Congo and over the years since independence? Then, while I was lost in my dark thoughts, I saw my storekeeper holding in his hand the jerry can that I had asked him for. I thought I was dreaming because I did not think that respect could still exist in a climate of such violence and such hatred. Yet, he handed it to me and told me calmly but cynically that they had killed all the Tutsis in the houses of the camp, and now they would kill my agronomist next door. I thought it was a bad dream and yet, I had before me a band of assassins ready to continue their despicable work, ready to continue their genocide. What a strange behavior characterized by my storekeeper, this man with two faces wanting to be respectful on one side and criminal on the other. The rebels were moving in front of the window. They were shouting and screaming but they did not stop. With their machetes, they forced a path through the cypress hedge separating the two houses and then headed to that of my agronomist. For the moment, death was only prowling around our little family. It was not our turn. The noise suddenly stopped. Then, suddenly, it started again and amplified. At the staccato rhythm of the singings was added the sound of stones hurled by the assailants on the tin roof, on the front door and on the windows of the house. The excitement was rising and the noise grew louder. Then, after half an hour, a great painful silence came down. It was the silence of the dead. For a while, we could not speak and did not know what to do. The minutes passed slowly, one after the other. An hour had passed and we were still surrounded by the overwhelming silence. Even the birds had stopped singing. Outside, there was no one in sight. I opened the door of the house and pricked up my ears. A scary bellowing, mournful and plaintive reached me, a roar from all the hills surrounding us. I did not understand its origin and it is only later that I understood. The Hutus in their killing spree moved from hill to hill in search of Tutsis to kill, and were burning their huts and cutting the hamstrings of their cows, which were the only wealth of Tutsis. The atrocious sounds would be followed by the slow agony of these animals, as they died bloodless.

I took a few steps in our garden and ventured towards the house of my agronomist, nothing in sight. I crossed the cypress hedge along the path taken by the rampaging column of men. Then I discovered the horror. On the doorstep, a pool of blood was flowing like a reddish river. My trusted agronomist was laying there, his head exploded, his body torn with machetes and spears. The atrocious unforgettable sight has marked me for many years, whose memory is forever indelible. I became an adult before my time. Inside the house whose door was closed, I heard crying. I knocked but no one came. The doors leading to the rooms remained closed. I learned later that day that my agronomist, who lived in the house with his wife and six children, had decided after half an hour of stones being thrown, to go out of the house to save his family. He was brutally murdered but his wife and children, although Tutsis were spared. My agronomist and the Tutsis in camp died for no reason but that of being born Tutsi. This is when my outlook on life changed and I realized that we often live in an illusion, while reality is quite different. I returned home, mentioned nothing to Nadine to prevent having her frightened, and lied down on the bed. I let loose my nerves and fell asleep. Around noon, I emerged from my restless sleep. The noise of the unfortunate cows probably dead and bloodless had disappeared and a heavy silence reigned. We did not know what to do. Should we take the jeep? How would we cross the river? Should we walk? Walking was madness as we would then be helpless if we were attacked. The hours passed and the situation did not change. We were stuck at the mercy of these murderers, these mass killers.

The entry to the garage reminiscent of sad memories

Around 5 p.m., the silence gave way to the sound of voices approaching the house. I left the house and recognized the police Captain of Muramvya accompanied by a dozen armed soldiers. They had left their vehicle in front of one of the broken bridges and had traveled on foot the distance separating the bridge from the houses. The Captain told me that once the Hutu rebels had accomplished their infamy in Teza and in the surrounding hills, they drove towards Muramvya, the cradle of the monarchy, hoping to take this city. The army had fortunately stopped them near Muramvya. Then, aware of what had happened in Teza, the captain decided to send a group of men to help us. This was the deliverance. However, this was only a partial deliverance. Indeed, they took with them women and children including the wife of my agronomist, his six children, Nadine and Eric. As for me, there was no room left in the vehicle waiting at the bottom of the hill! The Captain said he regretted having to temporarily leave Johnny and me on the spot but he would be back within one or two hours to get us. Therefore, I left Nadine whose behavior throughout this ordeal had been amazing. Indeed, she never showed signs of distress or of panic even as we separated. What self-control as she faced such extreme circumstances!

The small group then headed down the hill and I was left alone with Johnny. I was suddenly taken by doubts. Would I ever see Nadine and Eric again? The minutes passed and around 6 p.m., as is the case near the tropics, the darkness gradually enveloped the plantation, rendering it particularly lugubrious in this day of mourning. The rain fell as if the heavens shed tears on all these unnecessary deaths. What was I to do? Should I wait for the Captain or try to leave? I opted to wait for two to three hours and then leave on foot or by car. Indeed, I was afraid that the killers of my Tutsi staff and my agronomist that had been pushed back by the army would return into the plantation. My mind was full of gloomy thoughts. I was well aware that my life was in danger. It was clear to me that the Hutus and Batwas who had spared us in the morning might not continue to do so after being driven back by the army. I was an incriminating witness and eliminating me would be best for them. As for the drugged Pygmies, it was better not to be on their paths. Then, all of a sudden, I heard a death rattle coming from my jeep that I had left on the road bordering the house. I headed to my vehicle and saw with horror that my Tutsi driver had crawled behind the wheel and was dying with an arrow in the belly. His intestines were coming out of the horrible wound and he was breathing weakly. I could not do anything for him and he died soon after in horrible agony and groans. I withdrew his lifeless body from the jeep, laid him down on the side of the road and then went back to our house.

A Risky Gamble

Around 6:30 p.m., I decided not to stay in the house for fear of being surprised by the rebels. I went out with Johnny and walked a few feet to go hide in the ditch alongside the road. From there, I could better observe any movements. I held my dog near me to prevent him from barking or growling at the slightest noise because he was an ideal watchdog. We waited there until 8 p.m., expecting the police Captain to come and rescue us. However, though my life was at stake, he did not keep his promise and never came. In retrospect, it is my view that if anything would have happened to me, it would have been used by the Tutsis as a strong argument to demonstrate that the rebels had no mercy, neither for the Tutsis nor for the white and that, the follow-up killing spree of the Hutus by the Tutsis was even more justified. I was alone facing my own destiny not knowing what it will be and wondering what to do. However, I made up my mind: there is no way it is going to end here, and I would not die in this place on this night. Should I try to drive my jeep knowing that the bridges were cut off? Moreover, even if I could go through, what kind of peril was awaiting me during a night drive across burning huts with possible encounters with some drugged rebels? Even the army could, without hesitation, fire on a vehicle at night. Leaving was not without risks, but staying was not necessarily a better option. To go alone was obviously utopian. Therefore, I decided to come out of hiding and went around the nearby factory to see if I could get help from any survivors of the massacre. I carefully made the 100 yards separating me from the factory and at first saw nothing. A total silence reigned. I continued moving towards the camp and I discovered the horror, an unspeakable abomination. Death inflicted on me the horrible scenes of its dreadful deeds. Bloody corpses, skulls smashed with machetes. The only crime of these people was to have been born Tutsi. A common socio-cultural heritage became a crime punishable by capital punishment without trial. Their families, however, had been spared. Never had I witnessed such an outburst of violence. I was wondering how peaceful farmers can turn into ruthless killers? In the night, I returned slowly towards the factory and then suddenly faced a group of twenty men armed with the same spears, machetes and clubs that I had seen in the morning. My warehouseman was among them. Was this my last hour? Would they kill me? I did not know what to think. However, without losing my composure, I began to dialogue with those mutineers who confirmed that the army on the outskirts of Muramvya stopped them. What was I to say to this gang of murderers! I had no choice but to reveal my intention to leave the plantation and ask them if they wanted to accompany me because I needed assistance to eventually try to repair one of the bridges. Of course, it was a double-edged sword as I was the only witness of the massacre and they could prevent me from leaving, eliminating this inconvenient witness. However, they reacted quite unexpectedly, telling me again that the three bridges were cut and, therefore, impassable. They then told me that in any way they would not accompany me if I were to try something by myself. Indeed, even if we were successful in going through the first bridge, a second one leading to the main road was also cut. Therefore, the only option to avoid this second obstacle was to go through the forest path and drive about 6 miles in the eucalyptus forest in order to reach the main road. They told me they would not accompany me because the risk was too great to meet, on our way, some drugged Pygmies who would not hesitate to kill. I later learned that the Pygmies were paid the equivalent of one U.S. dollar–twice the daily wage of a worker –to kill a Tutsi. Therefore, an escape would be without being accompanied by the murderers of the entire Tutsi administrative staff of the plantation and of my agronomist.

I was about to return to our house when a group of ten Congolese came up to me. Most of them were working as mechanics in the plantation and only had working relationships with their Tutsi and Hutu colleagues. I unveiled my intentions and without hesitation, they offered to come with me and help me. I also told them that we would leave when everything seemed calm and went back to hide in my ditch. Around 10 p.m., I took my jeep and went down into the courtyard of the factory where the ten Congolese joined me. Then we headed to an unknown fate. The night was particularly dark because the stars are scarce at the beginning of the rainy season. We drove slowly with the lights off the slope leading us to the river whose depth was about 20 inches. The bridge that originally crossed over it was made of trunks of cypress trees, roughly 20 feet long and 13 feet wide. It was now effectively completely cut off and there were no other possible passages. We worked silently in total darkness for more than two hours to repair the bridge with four trunk halves of a width slightly larger than the wheels of our jeep. The crossing was hazardous but I had no choice. I had to cross over and take the risk to fall in the river. I stayed alone in the jeep and slowly engaged in the slope leading to the bridge. My heart tightened when I put the front wheels of the jeep on the trunks. Now, the most difficult part remained to be done and I was afraid that the trunks would move apart once all four tires were on them. The margin of error was limited because I could not deviate from the hollow formed by the two trunks joined together on the left side and separated from the two trunks placed on the right side by a gap of about 5 feet, corresponding to the width of my jeep. Finally, luck was on my side. Indeed, everything went perfectly until the front tires of the jeep left the trunks to engage the other side of the bridge. The slope was muddy and slippery and the front of the vehicle went slightly off course. As a result, one of the rear tires slipped off the trunk while its axle rested on the trunk. At the same time, the other tire was on the rounded part of the trunk and could have slipped off any moment. Fortunately, I had put the traction on all four wheels and activated the speed reducer. This allowed me to cross the few remaining feet. Everyone got back into the vehicle and then, still without lights, we took the trail through the thick eucalyptus forest. After half an hour of tense driving, we finally reached the main road linking Bujumbura to the border of Rwanda. I turned left to go to the town of Busangana (now Bukeye) located about nine miles away. We were alone in that dark night and the journey seemed endless. I finally arrived at the bazaar of the town of Busangana located at the intersection of the main road and then took the track leading to Muramvya. The road was slippery and the fog dense. Finally, I could feel the deliverance nearing as I saw the few lights of the city of Muramvya. The nightmare ended as I arrived at the house of our doctor friend and found Nadine and Eric. Since that dreadful day, nothing has managed to scare me except in my dreams. The next day we went down to Bujumbura where we stayed with friends for three months.

My Daily Visits to Teza

Given the conditions of insecurity that prevailed at Teza, I asked my employer if it was possible to be relocated, even temporarily in another station or plantation. My employer did not budge and told me that there was no other possibility of work, even temporary. He added that I had to go back to Teza as soon as possible or resign if I did not want to go. I did not really have the choice to resign, since my first objective was to ensure the future of our family and not get into the unknown. After discussing this issue with Nadine, we decided to stay in Burundi while exploring opportunities in other third-world countries. I told my employer that I had decided to keep my work at Teza and received instructions to resume my activities swiftly and make daily visits to Teza for a few hours for an unknown period of time. However, as soon as the situation would allow it, I would have to go back to Teza and stay there permanently. The security of the staff seemed rather secondary compared to meeting the objectives of the tea program and the financial windfall related to it. My managers obviously had to meet the objectives set by its contract with the European Community and demonstrate to the latter that everything was done to resume the tea operations as quickly as possible. Three days after our arrival in Bujumbura, a colleague and I, each armed with a 9 mm pistol produced by FN Herstal Belgium, went back to the plantation for a few hours. Our visits became daily inspections. We were going across this plantation empty of any soul to see if anything had been stolen or looted while trying to assess whether security conditions were improving. However, it is unrealistic to think that a few hours of daily visits and inspections can change the behavior of people who want to rob houses or steal equipment. Regarding the assessment of security conditions, it was equally utopian. Indeed, who could have predicted the ethnic cleansing of October 25 when everything was so quiet the day before, and how does one define safety criteria for a return to work? This daily round trip lasted two months. The drive alone consisted in going from about 2,300 feet to 7,500 feet in about 22 miles of steep spirals, and then driving about 12.4 miles of rough and slippery roads. These two months were grueling because of the difference in altitude going up and down the plantation. These were two months of constant tension when we circulated in plantations. To be on the lookout, always on the lookout, to see if there are potential attackers, was exhausting and nerve breaking. Our first visits were particularly difficult because many corpses littered the road. Some had been killed with knives and others had been shot. Unbearable was the sight and stench of these rotting corpses. The army had done its job of cleaning. Two weeks after the events, the rebellion was crushed and the authorities seemed to have the situation well in hand. Soldiers regularly visited the plantation and had set up a mortar on the platform of the plantation. They were shooting blindly into the forest because the insurgents were hiding there. There was lots of staging and a lot of noise for a few mortar rounds fired daily. After one week, the soldiers left Teza and returned to their barracks. The silence had fallen back on the plantation.

The Gruesome Discovery

Two weeks after the tragic events, I went back to Teza alone. I made, however, a detour, as I wanted to see the Captain in the town of Muramvya and tell him how disgusted I was by his lack of commitment and failure from an authority to render assistance to a person in danger. I knew that the Captain would find any excuse to justify his gruesome behavior. However, I also knew that silence is the worst, most damaging kind of feedback. Six miles before arriving there, I saw in a curve at the foot of a cliff many bodies. I stopped, got off my jeep and noticed with horror bodies riddled with bullets. All of them were the bodies of the killers of my Hutu employees who had fomented the rebellion in the plantation. Among them, I also recognized some vegetable vendors from the Kavumu Spring. Their presence intrigued me. I learned later that my agronomist who was brutally murdered had stopped at this spring to buy some vegetables the night before returning home. Among the sellers were some of his killers who were arrested and summarily executed without trial by the police. I counted 35 bodies robbed of their meager possessions. The stench of the corpses already baked by the sun and covered with flies that penetrate the skin like dust made me feel sick. I was so upset by the turn of events and decided that it might be better not to have an argument with the Captain that day. I had the opportunity later. Still today, 50 years after these tragic events, I sometimes wake up at night from nightmares in which I live again all these moments and tragedies that I witnessed. I often think back about that column of men going up the hill to perpetrate their crimes, about the radio button allowing me to communicate with Bujumbura and the death threat associated with it, about the bloody bodies of my staff and about their assassins. This is why this wonderful source of Kavumu remains forever in my memory as the source of good and evil. It represents good through this nourishing land producing vegetables and beautiful flowers; and it represents evil embodied by these two-faced vendors, smiling and affable one-day, and bloodthirsty murderers the next day. This is also why in my mind I cannot dissociate such pure and limpid water flowing from the Kavumu Spring from the one I imagined tinged with crimson blood that tragic morning of October 25, 1965. We will see later in this book that these tragic events that plunged Burundi into mourning in 1965 were only heralding the beginnings of intensely dreary tomorrows for this tiny country.

The Premonition

A month after the events during one of my daily visits to the plantation, I was about to leave the main road to take on my left the road to the plantation. An old woman was waiting at the fork and waived her hand suggesting she wanted to speak with me. Intrigued, I stopped. She said in Kirundi, which I mastered a little bit at the time, not to go to the plantation because my life would be endangered. I asked her to explain herself and she said that she learned that the rebels would wait for me near the plantation to kill me! I was skeptical and did not believe her, so I decided to continue driving. I drove the few miles separating me from the hill where the factory and houses were located and parked the jeep near our house. I was worried and watchful, yet fully decided to ward off evil. I got off my vehicle and went towards the nearby factory. Not a soul. Not a sound. I was alone, all alone in the plantation where a few weeks ago more than two thousand men and women worked. The silence, always the silence. I searched the bottom of the hill and around it, but saw nothing suspicious. I was reassured and told myself at that moment that I had done well not to listen to this woman and to continue my ride. I took the road again, drove a few miles in the plantation and then came back to the factory. Suddenly, I looked again down the hill and saw two dozen men slowly walking up towards the factory. My blood froze because it reminded me of the column of men going up to the factory to commit their crimes one month before. There was no doubt that history was repeating itself. These men were without a doubt coming to execute what this brave woman told me they would. I watched it again and realized that they were armed with machetes and spears! It obviously was not for pleasure. I ran to my jeep and drove down the hill, hoping the main bridge was intact. As I came close to it, my heartbeat went up--the trunks had been moved again and the bridge was impassable. I had no choice. I had to cross the river at all costs, passing on the sides of the bridge. In a few seconds, I identified a place that seemed most suitable for this crossing. Then, I put the traction on all four wheels, put it in lower first gear and went down slowly in the river already swollen by the rains. About 1.6 feet of water came into the cabin and flooded the lower part of the engine. My valiant jeep coughed a little in the middle of the river but once more proved to be a perfect all-terrain vehicle and allowed me to reach the other side of the bank. I was saved *in extremis*. Once again, death had only prowled around me! Upon my return to Bujumbura, I informed my direction of the assassination attempt. Though they seemed quite concerned about the turn of events, they did not alter in any way the pace of visits! To alleviate the risk, however, they made sure that a few soldiers would accompany me for several days. As to Nadine, I did not mention anything of my eventful day to not frighten her unnecessarily. The next day, I went back to Teza with a few soldiers that I had picked up at Muramvya. They helped me make temporary repairs to the bridge.

The next day, they brought with them a dozen prisoners from the prison of Muramvya to fix the bridge permanently. During the following days, they continued to escort me to ensure my safety. Soon they stated that the situation had returned to normal and that it was no longer necessary for them to come along with me. Therefore, I resumed my daily solitary visits.

A Gradual Return to Normal

My daily and usually solitary round trips lasted two and a half months, until the end of 1965. At each visit, I expected that our house would be ransacked and emptied, as were the other two neighboring houses and the many houses repeatedly looted and vandalized in the nearby Congo. Yet, with the exception of a broken window in the bedroom of Eric that probably served as a temporary shelter to a mutineer, nothing had been stolen, nothing had been vandalized. To date, I have only one explanation for this surprising behavior since poverty or enmity of some workers among the two thousand who were employed could justify theft or vandalism. However, while I acknowledge being uncompromising on principles of discipline, I think I have never shown any injustice to the workers. Without being sure of this, it is possible that this behavior towards us was the manifestation of a certain respect from a population still very different from the neighboring Congo.

Of course, during our stay in Bujumbura I analyzed employment opportunities in other emerging markets given the climate of insecurity that still reigned in the interior of Burundi. I received a strong offer to go run a tea plantation in Madagascar. However, I declined the offer because the plantation was totally isolated and located eight hours of track away from Antananarivo, the capital of Madagascar.

Then, finally the tension decreased in Burundi and in Teza and the meetings I made during my daily visits with a growing number of plantation workers convinced me that it would be possible to resume work soon in Teza, even if the danger was of course not excluded. Just over two months after the tragic events of October, my management decided that the conditions were back to almost normal at Teza and that work could resume. This assessment was, of course, very subjective since the visits of my direction to Teza were rather rare. I had no choice, however, but to go back to Teza with my family or leave ISABU and reach out to a very uncertain future. Nadine and I decided to stay in Burundi.

VII. BACK TO THE PLANTATION

Plate of Teza

Another Challenge

January 1966. Earlier this month, the whole family went back to Teza and I resumed my activities. We were the only Europeans isolated on our hill. The working conditions and the political context were particularly difficult and tension was almost permanent. My gun did not leave me wherever I was, be it in the plantation or at night under my pillow at hand's reach. I had to rebuild from scratch the hiring of qualified staff since I had no agricultural engineers, no accountants, no typists, no secretaries and no warehousemen. All of them had been killed or vanished. In addition, during the first two months, I only had a few workers available. When I asked about the reasons for this absenteeism, the workers unanimously mentioned that it was because of the fear of reprisals by the army that came regularly to the plantation to assess the situation and, of course, work out a show of force and hold random firing towards the forest. They also told me that many of the workers they knew disappeared. This point was undeniable and I could easily verify the truth by noting that a third of the workers who were on the old payroll, about 700 people, never returned to work or collected their salary for the dreadful month of October. I guess they died during the terrible reprisals from the loyalist troops that followed the Hutu coup or they may have fled to neighboring countries. I also found it very difficult to recruit workers who were willing to accompany me in the forest and help me in the identification and demarcation of land suitable for tea production. Indeed, most workers feared the Pygmies who retreated in the forest to avoid the risk of being killed by the army, and thought they were a constant danger. As for me, it was useless to spend too much time analyzing things. Even if my fears were real, the work had to move forward. During the daytime, I was continually on the alert and at night, I practiced shooting in my yard. This practice was not really to enhance my skills but to reassure me, even if this reassurance was an illusion. I thought rather naïvely that making it known that I was armed would deter potential aggressors. Yet, I knew full well that a revolver against spears, machetes and drugged rebels would be worthless. Gradually, however, the working conditions improved and the tension subsided. This work in the bush where everything had to be done made me discover the beauty of being an agronomist. In parallel, the difficult conditions we faced during the first two years of our stay in Burundi led me to appreciate the importance and the richness of a united family. I also discovered a lifestyle and above all an environment that allowed me to blossom. I had every intention of throwing my anchor in this two-faced country, this land of joys and sorrows--violent and yet charming--since it was the harbor my heart had elected.

Political Developments

Since the coup of October 1965 failed in Bujumbura and inside the country, the Tutsi government and army carried out the purge of many Hutu civilians and military leaders. The plantation had not been spared and the arrests and disappearances have been many. The dead numbered in the thousands. However, national and international news had little to say about this selective genocide. Indeed, Burundi being a poor and little known country without resources, the international media had no interest in the recent events. On the national level, the press was heavily censored.

Yet, I think this failed coup and the terrible reprisals perpetrated later by the army were significant in the development of the massacres that would devastate the country over the following decades. The Tutsi military officer in charge of the so-called operations of pacification, Major Michel Micombero, was quickly offered a ministerial position in the government. Mwami Mwambutsa fled to Europe in early 1966 and never returned. However, he refused to abdicate. Therefore, the daily administration became the responsibility of a mixed assemblage of elements of the army, of civilians and young people, most of them of Tutsi origin. This group began using Prince Charles Ndizeye, the youngest son of King Mwambutsa, hoping that if the succession crisis was resolved in his favor, it would allow them a new entry in politics. This is precisely what happened. On July 8, 1966, the 19-year-old Prince Ndizeye was proclaimed the new head of state. The next day, Prince Ndizeye fired Prime Minister Leopold Biha, suspended the constitution and asked Major Micombero to form a new government. On September 1, 1966 in Muramvya, Ndizeye was proclaimed Mwami of Burundi under the dynasty of Ntare V. His reign was, however, very short and he was the last Mwami in Burundi. The following months witnessed indeed a rapid deterioration of the relations between the Mwami and those who assisted him in becoming King. On November 28, 1966, while attending the first anniversary of the takeover of Mobutu in Kinshasa, he learned by radio that the army had overthrown him and that a republic had been proclaimed with Major Micombero as the first President at the age of 26. A curfew was established from 6 p.m. to 6 a.m. throughout the territory for an indefinite period. Thus ended a monarchy said to have lasted more than 300 years. It also ended the shortest reign of the defunct monarchy. Subsequently, the Tutsis remained in power for 21 years.

We are Four

September 21, 1966. On this day, our family was enlarged by the birth of a lovely blond girl named Karin. At the great pride of her father, she was exhibiting the characteristic Nordic features of her paternal grandmother. While a major landslide almost prevented me from attending the birth of our son Eric, in the case of our daughter it was an earthquake, fortunately small-scale and leading only to minor damages, that marked the day of her birth. It was a very strange coincidence that this birth was preceded by a quake because the Burundian custom states that an earthquake always announces a great event. We relived this delicious moment of love, tenderness and intimacy that we had at the birth of Eric. History repeated itself and we were thrilled. Outside, the first rains had awakened the earth surface parched by the sun and nature bestowed us with ravishing flowers, while recently hatched birds seemed to share our joy with their various songs. A few hours after the birth of Karin, I headed back to the post office as I had done two and a half years ago to share our happiness with the parents of Nadine and my father by sending a telegram, a forgotten means of communication nowadays, but so precious at that time. A few days later, we were back on our hill where Eric and Karin thrived in contact with the surrounding rich nature.

Telegram

Inauguration of the Teza Tea Factory

In late 1966, the tea factory of Teza became functional and was inaugurated with great pomp by President Micombero. He arrived by helicopter and was greeted by Intore drummers and dancers. Later on, he solemnly proceeded to inaugurate the factory by cutting the ribbon. Then, the first tealeaves plucked from tea bushes planted in late 1963 were turned into black tea. This tea quickly became one of the best-quoted teas on the London market.

Helicopter of President Micombero

President Micombero visiting Teza

In the Land of Joys and Sorrows

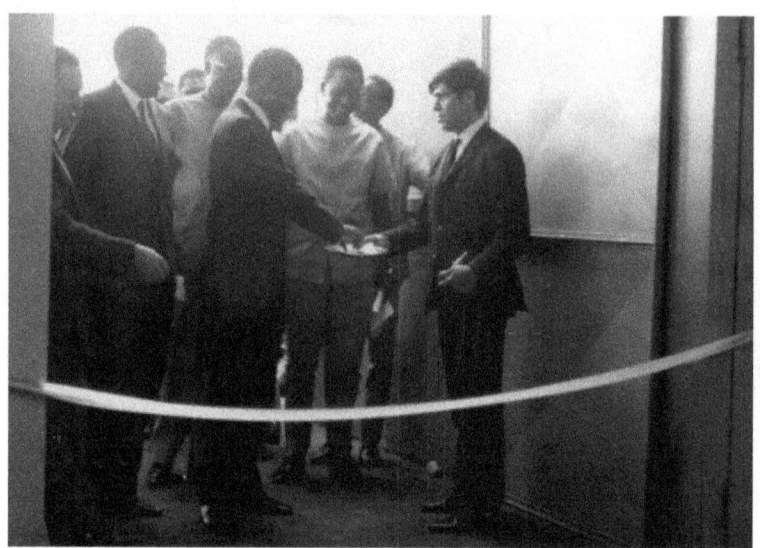
Visit of President Micombero for the inauguration of the Teza tea factory

Intuition

July 1967. As for all monthly statements, the accounting department was preparing the plantation's payroll for approximately 2,000 workers. It was an arduous and complex task because we had to transcribe all the names from the muster rolls of each work team on a large registry and indicate the salary and the number of days worked. This work required about one week because the entire transcript was done manually. Three days before the payroll, I realized that a major fraudulent attempt had been made. My new Tutsi chief accountant had simply established a payroll made payable to more than 300 fictitious names. I made the decision to fire him immediately and to start the entire task over. This led to an additional week of work and control which delayed the payment by three days to the great discontent of the workers. Some had become arrogant and aggressive and the tension grew. There were, however, no notable incidents. On payday, I settled into the back of the shed adjacent to the factory with the bookkeepers while the workers lined up in columns in the hangar in front of our tables. The payment began and we moved on one call at a time, enumerating the number of days worked and the wages to be received. Then, the workers would sign their payroll, usually with the fingerprint of their thumb soaked with ink, as the vast majority was illiterate. Two hours had passed without incidents. Suddenly, I saw the accountant whom I had fired three days earlier slip in among the workers and go behind my table. He told me that he was just coming to pick up his personal affairs because he was unable to do it when he was let go. I was focused on monitoring the payroll and found the explanation plausible. At first, I did not pay much attention to his request. However, I was on my guard. Was it my sixth sense?--It is highly likely. While I continued to distribute the payments, that sixth sense probably saved my life. Suddenly, I turned my head for no apparent reason except that of being guided by intuition. And this is when I saw my accountant, arm raised with a heavy hammer. He was about to smash my head. I avoided the blow, grabbed his arm and twisted it to remove the hammer. We wrestled violently and rolled on the ground. Swift as a heel, he tried to escape and to grab his hammer that had fell on the ground. The fight quickly escalated, but I ended up taking over. For once, my two years of practice in amateur boxing helped me out of the ring. I pounded his face with my fists; his blood squirted and splattered my shirt as I continued punching him. No one around intervened and the workers remained impassive. Finally, I let him go and he ran away. The next day, I filed a complaint with the police of the city of Muramvya for fraud and attempted murder. My accountant was arrested and imprisoned for a short while. He was released after ten days because none of the workers testified seeing him with a hammer risen above my head. Of course, I was the only one who saw this criminal act and my complaint was therefore quickly dismissed due to lack of evidence! It was quite logical because in the political context of the time, a Hutu worker would never have testified against a Tutsi for fear of retaliation by the provincial authorities and army composed mainly of Tutsis. October 1965 was still too fresh in the memory.

The Mimic Gift of Monkeys

At the edge of the Kibira Forest, we established a nursery near the river in order to irrigate it. Seedling tea plants remained generally between 18 months and two years in the nursery before being extracted for planting. Prior to planting, which was bare-root, the plants had to be cut down, a procedure called coppicing. Coppicing involves cutting the plants about 8 inches above ground level and extracting them. Then, a tractor takes them to the planting site.

The procedure of coppicing fascinated many monkeys that lived in the forest. They used to watch us while swinging from one branch to another in the nearby trees and making their particular laughter-like sounds. They most probably wanted to tell us something, but the language barrier was a major obstacle! Then, one morning I realized too late, what they wanted to tell us. Indeed, after we stopped working the day before around 3 p.m., they came down from their observation sites to visit the nursery where they dutifully peeled the plants just like they do with bananas, leaving in the ground a stump 4 to 6 inches tall. In their way, they made us aware that they too could do the job that did not seem too complex for them!

Karin and the German Shepherd

November 1968. Since the resumption of work in early 1966, we had on our hill, as our only neighbors, a Dutch couple whose husband worked with me as the head of the tea factory of Teza. In September 1968, they went to Europe for a period of two months for their holidays. During that period, we took care of their German shepherd, a beautiful two year-old male weighing well over 90 pounds. Our daughter Karin who was two years old was thrilled because she had found a docile playmate that never showed any hostility towards her. The two months passed without any problems and when its masters came back, the dog returned to their home. The latter, once occupied by my savagely murdered agronomist, was separated from ours by a simple cypress hedge that could easily be crossed. A few days after the return of our neighbors, the drama occurred. The night was falling and suddenly we had a visit from our neighbor with Karin bleeding in her arms. Her lower face, neck and torso were so completely red that we imagined the worst. The blood continued to flow from a wound located in the neck but we could not locate it accurately. Our neighbor told us with distraught that Karin had crossed the fence and that her shepherd had suddenly jumped at her for no apparent reason and had severely bitten her on the throat. Luckily, she was near the dog at the time of the attack and she could control it instantly. She then administered first aid to Karin by pouring an entire bottle of mercurochrome on her neck and face while putting a bandage to try to stop the bleeding. I went berserk and my first reaction was to grasp the poker and go kill the dog. However, I changed my mind, took Karin in my arms and put her in my car. Then, I headed to the hospital in Bujumbura. I never went down the escarpment leading to Bujumbura so fast. Arriving at the hospital around 8 p.m., the emergency service immediately called the only surgeon at the hospital and in Bujumbura, whom we knew well since he had delivered Karin. After having evaluated her, he told me that she had been very lucky because the shepherd had indeed bitten her in the neck and his teeth made a large wound located 0.08 inches away from the carotid! 0.08 inches more and the carotid would have been cut, leaving Karin little chance of survival given the impossibility of any emergency medical treatment in the bushes. The surgeon finally decided not to stitch the wound to minimize scarring but joined the two lips of the wound with tape--surprising but wonderful. The effect was immediate, the blood stopped flowing and an hour after our arrival at the hospital we were ready to go back in our bushes. Nadine and our neighbors were waiting for us with obvious anxiety. I reassured them and a few days later the memory of the near-fatal attack had already faded away. We may wonder what happened. Most likely, this attack was made by revolt against the submissive attitude that the dog had displayed towards Karin during its stay with us. It is quite possible that Karin slightly went overboard when playing with the dog. Dogs are pack animals and social relations are based entirely on the report of dominance; from dominated by a child when he was at our home, the dog reassumed its dominance when it returned to its home and rebelled at the first opportunity. Following this accident, the hedge separating the two houses has been consolidated to avoid another meeting between the dog and Karin. Once this moment of fright faded away, our lives fertile in events in the bushes resumed, while Eric and Karin continued to flourish without major concerns in this extraordinary universe.

In the Land of Joys and Sorrows

Our place with Eric and Karin

Karin

Back to the Plantation

Karin

Karin

The Flight over the Plantation in DC3

January 1969. In the late sixties, the French government had offered the government of Burundi a Caravelle, one of the most successful European first generation jetliners as a presidential plane and a DC3 Dakota. Two poisoned gifts for a country that did not have the financial resources to ensure the maintenance of these aircrafts and to fly them on a regular basis. France therefore provided maintenance and flying. I knew the French military pilot who was responsible for flying the old DC3 a number of hours per month. As he was looking for new flight plans, I suggested flying over the Zaire-Nile because the sky was clear at the beginning of the short dry season and then heading down to the plantation in Teza. Thing said thing done, and here we were flying at the expense of France towards the famous Zaire-Nile Crest and the plantation in Teza. I was a theoretical co-pilot so that I could film the best shoots, as we would fly over the plantation. We first flew low over the Zaire-Nile Crest located at an altitude of about 7,500 feet where strong turbulence prevailed at all times. Then, we flew along it for about 30 minutes almost up to the Rwandan border, before turning back towards Teza. This seasoned pilot flew with cold feet several times over it at a very low altitude. The scenery was fascinating. Flying over Teza lost in the heart of the forest made me fully embrace what this forest and the plantation meant to me. This forest with its beauty as it has been for a millennia and as it was our world for seven years, this forest with its irrefutable materiality and sedentary, and the tea plantation with the splendor of its characteristic green hue and its sweet melancholy. This impressive flight will remain forever embedded in my memory because it reminds me that I had been extremely fortunate during my stay in Teza to live within a world of animals and plants extinct for many of us.

Fly over Teza – View of the houses

Our Hunting Night in the Province of Kirundo

August 1969. We decided with a couple of very good friends, Hector and Martha, living in Bugarama, 9.3 miles from Teza, to enjoy the long dry season and go hunting at night in Kirundo. This province consists of a plateau with an elevation below 5,250 feet. It is located in northern Burundi and shares the border with the Republic of Rwanda. Although being a heavily populated province, the population was then very unevenly distributed. In less populated areas, the fauna was extremely rich and diverse and included a large number of antelopes. These antelopes are herbivores and at the time were causing significant damage to local people's traditional cultures, which led them to a constant hunting. Crop yield was very low and any loss of harvest due to uncertain weather or damage by predators could be catastrophic during the lean season, or hunger gap. This period corresponds to the dry season and is a time during which the whole family lives on reserves from storerooms until the first harvests of the rainy season.

In the Land of Joys and Sorrows

Map of Burundi - Kirundo Province

From Teza, we made the trip with two cars, and after about seven hours on bumpy and dusty roads, we arrived at Kirundo in the early evening. I left my car there. It was a Fiat 124 coupe, which is a rather unsuitable vehicle for small tracks and especially for ruts. After a light meal in a small restaurant run by Indians, practically the only foreign community in this small town, we got into the VW Beetle of our friends, best suited for the small vehicle tracks that we were to follow. Their car was equipped with a fixed roof. This roof was fairly rudimentary but it would play a crucial role in our night hunting. Indeed, to identify the animals' eyes we decided together that Nadine would settle on the roof of the VW with a powerful light beam to illuminate the savannah of acacia and shrubs. Such exercise was not without risk because she had to hold the lamp in one hand, cling to the roof with the other hand since the vehicle was moving, and upon seeing the eyes of an animal, she had to let go of the roof to tap thrice on the body of the car, which meant stopping the vehicle immediately. Then, she had to keep the beam pointed at the animal to allow the hunter to identify whether they were youngsters or carrying mothers, which were of course excluded from the hunt. Hector was a good hunter while I was only an apprentice. He knew perfectly well how to make this distinction but needed the assistance of Nadine. At his request, the beam of light needed to be lowered or on the contrary raised, or brought to the right or left to better gage the dimension of the animal and identify the possibility of a carrying mother. Hector's requests were transmitted by a knock from inside the vehicle to the roof according to a code on which we agreed--one knock meant to raise the beam, two to lower it, three to move to the left and four to move it to the right. When Hector was satisfied, he would get out of the vehicle and try to shoot the animal. Sometimes of course, the animal, not fooled, would take advantage of these changes in orientation of the beam to penetrate into the darkness of the night and the whole scenario had to start over.

Without any breaks, our hunting continued all night and when dawn broke, we had killed six antelopes and a porcupine. While the six antelopes were part of the hunting bag of Hector, I did shoot the porcupine but not without a great fear. Indeed, shortly before dawn, while the six antelopes had already been shot, Nadine spotted another pair of eyes and Hector told me that it was my turn. The vehicle stopped and I started moving into the shrubby savannah. I had taken a few steps but could not see anything. On the other hand, I heard a sound that was totally unknown to me, like a rattling sound accompanied by grunts. I was not reassured. I took a few steps toward the sound and then everything happened very quickly. All of a sudden, I saw in the darkness a brown-black body extended with long black and white spines that were up to 16 to 19 inches tall. I immediately fired and this is how I was lucky. I had just shot a porcupine whose behavior is very interesting when defending itself. Of course, I learned about the behavior of this animal after the hunt and it would have been better if I knew about it before to avoid unpleasant surprises. Indeed, a porcupine stops when a predator approaches and if touched its sharp spines break off and fall into the skin of the predator. After a short wait, the porcupine may even pounce on the predator, thrust its thorns in the body of the assailant, and inflict in this way extremely painful wounds prone to infections caused by germs that are on the quills. The quills have tiny backward facing barbs that catch on the skin, keep the quills firmly implanted, and render their extraction both difficult and painful. Next time when I hear a rattling sound in the bushes, I'll know what to do and what not to do! By 7 a.m., we were exhausted after this long sleepless night. However, this was nothing compared to our brave pilot who remained throughout the night perched on a fixed roof more appropriate to put suitcases on than a person. After a well-deserved breakfast stop, we took the long way back home.

On our way to Kirundo

The VW and its rudimentary luggage rack

Last stop before the hunt

Refueling

Off to the hunt

The old man

New Attempt or Simulacrum of a Coup

September 1969. Right after we came back from our famous night hunt, we learned that the government had discovered the attempt of a new coup orchestrated by the Hutu and scheduled for September 16 and 17, 1969. It is difficult to say if it was a real attempt or merely a pretext for a purge among the Hutus of the government and army. While many Hutu soldiers were summarily executed, numerous arrests ensued. Twenty Hutus from the government and the army were tried and sentenced to death on December 18 for conspiring against the state security. They were executed two days later. According to some sources, about 100 executions were carried out during the month of December. Whatever the figure, it was clear that the Tutsi supremacy was reinforcing its position. Seven of the twelve ministers were now Tutsis and they occupied the key positions of External Affairs, Interior Affairs, Defense and Security. Additionally, six of the eight provincial governors were also Tutsi. However, this new Hutu purge after the one of 1965 further created a radical Hutu movement that triggered another coup in 1972, which I mention later in this book.

In the Land of Joys and Sorrows

VIII. BUJUMBURA

My New Assignment

September 1970. In early 1970, I managed to negotiate with my director a new assignment at the Agricultural Research Station of Imbo, located 15.5 miles north of Bujumbura. This new assignment allowed us to live in Bujumbura starting in September 1970 and initiate the schooling of Eric and Karin until the houses to be built on the station were completed. We knew that our stay in the city would necessarily be short-lived as the various buildings were to be completed in early 1972, and we would then have to live at my new workplace.

My assignment to the Imbo Station was a new professional challenge for me. Indeed, cultures of altitudes, the bushes and the cool and rainy subtropical climate that was our universe for seven years were part to the past. I was now faced with the tropical climate of the hot dry Imbo plain whose altitude varies between 2,540 and 3,280 feet, while the average temperature was around 95°F in the day and did not drop below 70°F overnight. The station was the logistical support of a large irrigated rice field of 12,350 acres and of cotton culture in the region. Its research program mainly focused on these two cultures and on soil improvement. While waiting for the housing, the infrastructure of the station consisted of a modest office, a small laboratory and a warehouse.

We were, however, dreading our future move because the climate and health conditions of the plain were extremely difficult. Indeed, due to its tropical-disease-friendly hot and damp climate, this region was quite unoccupied until the end of the 19th century. In fact, there was even a legend that claimed that if a Mwami were to see the Lake Tanganyika, he would die. The heat was debilitating in the plain, mosquitoes were abundant and schistosomiasis, the world second parasitic endemic after malaria, reigned in irrigated or flooded zones. It was impossible to stand outside after sunset because the mosquitoes were kings and terribly aggressive. Moreover, the high temperature at night certainly did not make the nights more enjoyable. At that time, there were obviously no talks about air conditioning. Finally, even if the distance between Bujumbura and the station was only 15.5 miles, the last 9.5 miles leading to the station consisted of a bumpy and dusty road giving little incentive to travel. Living on site would mean that Nadine would have to make four trips per day, or 124 miles, including 75 miles of tracks to drive our children to the school in Bujumbura and pick them up afterwards. To spend about four hours on empty roads in scorching heat and in a fine dust that seeped into the car easily with of course no air conditioning, was totally unthinkable from the points of view of health and security. Finally, to settle in the plains in spartan and difficult conditions after having already experienced the bushes for seven years, was certainly not, what we aspired for. Nadine and I were thus faced with a terrible dilemma because we both knew, even if we avoided the topic of a possible move, that we could not handle living in this inhospitable plain. We also knew that we would have to face the unknown and the difficulties in finding a job if we decided to return to Belgium. Fortunately, many problems delayed the construction of homes that were not completed until mid-1974. However, we decided to return to Belgium when the constructions would be completed rather than face the difficult living conditions and the sensitivity to our health, not to mention the unacceptable conditions of schooling. The Research Station and the Imbo plain were therefore my professional world from early 1971 to September 1974, while Bujumbura was our new family and social universe. How fortunate for the Bushmen that we had been for seven years to finally be in a city with its civilization, restaurants, social life, and the pleasures of many sporting activities in Bujumbura and at the Lake Tanganyika. Unfortunately, our stay in Bujumbura would be tarnished by the terrible genocide of 1972. As I mention later in this book, it will leave an indelible mark in my memory.

First Contact with the United States

Our stay in Bujumbura began rather oddly, which can be interpreted in various ways. Some claim that the car accident that Nadine had was entirely fortuitous, while others say that this accident was a premonitory sign of what the future held in store for us. Indeed, after returning to Belgium at the end of my assignment at the Imbo Station in September 1974 and spending six years in Belgium, I was hired in late 1980 by the World Bank in Washington, D.C., United States, which is the country were we stayed since the end of my career in early 2002. Then what meaning can we draw from Nadine's first exploration of the American territory in late 1970 when she returned home after driving the children to school? We were staying then in a house that was contiguous with that of the U.S. Embassy. At that time, there were no special security and a concrete barrier did not surround the Embassy. Additionally, the sloping yard of the Embassy was not isolated from the entrance to our garage. The only demarcation between the gardens of two properties consisted in a bank and a small wooden fence. Nadine was relatively new at driving a vehicle, as she was driving on a regular basis for about two months. One day upon coming back home, she turned into the alley of our garage while driving rather quickly. She must have had a moment of confusion in the handling of the pedals. Rather than pushing on the brake pedal to avoid smashing into the wall at the end of the garage, she pushed on the acceleration pedal while keeping the car in the direction of the yard of the Embassy. The results were immediate since the car, after going through the bank and the barrier separating the two yards went through the slope of the yard of the Embassy and finally stopped in a flat area against another bank. Nadine, shocked, remained a moment in the car while Madam Ambassador alerted by the strange noise, came hastily out of her house, saw Nadine emerging unscathed from the car, and exclaimed,, "Oh my god, that's so funny to see a car in my garden!" When I came back late afternoon from work and saw the car heavily damaged in the yard of our neighbor, I became anxious not knowing what to expect. Fortunately, after pushing the front door of our house my fears immediately went away as I saw Nadine unharmed, but sorry for the car we had just acquired. I reassured her and told her to start driving my car immediately. I asked her to drive to town with me so that her fears could be dispelled. At first, she refused, then after a few minutes, she finally took the wheel and everything ran beautifully. Her confidence had returned. As for her car, chassis bent, it was good for scrap. However, in Africa, miracles are made with cars and everything can be repaired. We had an acquaintance who taught at the Mechanic School of Bujumbura and he was looking for damaged vehicles so that students can try their hand at practical work. It is in their hands that Nadine's car was put back together. However, the sequels of the accident, despite a new paint, were still visible and the car had a notorious tendency to steer to the left. This was more than likely a souvenir of that left turn taken a little bit too cheerfully by Nadine! These defects were by no means prohibitive for the reintegration in the local traffic where dilapidated and dangerous vehicles were the norm. On the other hand, I never thought we could have sold our car at a very decent price to an Embassy. You may say that experience is obviously important and when a vehicle has had the opportunity to be introduced within an Embassy, in this case the U.S. Embassy, such vehicle finds it easier to sell its merits to another Embassy. This was indeed the case as Nadine's vehicle was sold to another Embassy, which shall remain nameless for reasons of discretion after passing the inspection in the hands of the expert mechanic of the same Embassy!

In the Imbo plain with the car being repaired

Tanganyika Lake

How can I describe this fascinating lake, the dives I made in it and the permanent dangers that characterize it without briefly introducing Lake Tanganyika (see Appendix 1).

The context

Lake Tanganyika borders Burundi for 93 miles. Covering a total area of 12,702 square miles, it is slightly larger than Belgium and roughly the same size as the state of Maryland, U.S., where we reside. The Burundian zone represents about 8% of this area, with the remainder split between the Democratic Republic of Congo (45%), Tanzania (41%) and Zambia (6%). Formed during the Miocene about 20 million years ago, Lake Tanganyika is the oldest lake in the African Rift Valleys. Worldwide, it is the seventh lake by area and the second lake by depth. It reaches in places a depth of 4,708 feet! These unusual dimensions make this lake the largest reservoir of fresh water in Africa, while representing 18% of the world's fresh water.

Wildlife[27]

Lake Tanganyika contains a particularly rich and diversified halieutic fauna in the benthic and coastal areas. This diversity is actually similar to the one encountered in oceans. Among the fauna represented are nearly 300 species. About two-thirds of these fishes are endemic. The most notorious ones are the Nile Perch (*Lates niloticus*), also known as the Sangala, the Mukeke (*Lates stappersii*), the African Catfish or Clarias (also known as the Silures) and the Tilapia, introduced into the Congo in 1950. In the crevices offered by the rocky environment, there is also the dangerous aquatic Naja, also called the water cobra. At the entrance of estuaries, we encounter the extremely poisonous globefish, also known as the puffer fish. Finally, crocodiles and hippos are especially common. This rich fauna is an irresistible attraction to those fond of underwater exploration.

My Dives in the Lake

Passionate about scuba diving since the age of 13 and about Oceanography when I was in High School, I have had the opportunity to dive in several seas. On the other hand, I've never been diving in lakes. Lake Tanganyika provided me the opportunity. This wonderful lake of fabulous richness encompasses several unique dive sites. However, some of these sites can also be dangerous for the divers due to the potential presence of crocodiles wallowing along the shores lined with thick vegetation, but also due to water cobra. Despite the potential danger that requires constant vigilance and an appropriate choice of diving

---

[27] Lévêque, Christian; Paugy, Didier. *Les poissons des eaux continentales africaines*. [Fishes from African Inland Waters]

sites, I have lived exceptional dives. I made several dives, each rivaling in beauty, one with the others and displaying funds very rich in wildlife. The lake has some outstanding diving sites, which I have visited many times. Among them, there is the site of Magara located near Minago, 26 miles south of Bujumbura. A sandy beach provides easy access to the water and after a few feet; you can dive along a drop or slab that slopes gently up to 180 feet. Diving along this drop provides an amazing sensation of weightlessness and immensity. It is impossible to distinguish the bottom, which is lost in a deep blue. Diving without seeing the bottom gives you a sensational feeling of freedom. It can also be quite stressful but it is always very uplifting. Another extraordinary site is the one marked by a buoy in the middle of the lake. It was also not without apprehension that I dove from the boat to slowly slip into an abysmal emptiness. Indeed, the dive is done without landmarks and relies only on a compass. Then, at a depth of 98 to 131 feet, the tip of a huge rock mass can be seen. It starts at about 164 feet and then disappears into the abyss of the lake. This scenery takes your breath away, not only because of its beauty but also because of the wildlife that inhabits this dream place.

During my dives, I had the opportunity to meet several times the one called the 'Emperor Cichlid'[28] (*Boulengerochromis microlepis*). This predatory fish is the largest in the family of Cichlids and second in the world after the South American 'Giant Peacock Bass' (*Cichla temensis*). It can reach a size of 27.5 inches and those I encountered were nearly 24 inches long. This is an extremely captivating and majestic fish of yellow-gold colors and brown-green vertical stripes. I never grew tired of looking at them and those I met seemed oblivious of my presence. Another majestic Cichlid often met in small groups is the 'Fairy Cichlid' (*Neolamprologus brichardi*). It has a maximum size of about 4 inches and presents graceful filaments on its fins. This fish is marketed under the name of 'Princess of Burundi' and it bears its name beautifully. What a sight to remember. I also saw frequently the 'Hunchback of Tanganyika' (*Cyphotilapia frontosa*). This Cichlid grows up to 10 inches and presents a white or blue color marked with six black vertical stripes. It is a wonder that one can never grow tired of

---

[28] This large family includes between 1,600 and 1,800 species of fish living mainly in Africa, Central and South America, along the coasts of India and Sri Lanka, and in the Middle East. The size of these fishes varies from a few inches for dwarf cichlids to nearly 3.5 feet. Some specimens are highly prized by aquarists.

watching. These fantastic dives also include encounters with catfishes and with the huge schools of Lake Tanganyika sprats (*Stolothrissa tanganyikae*), often called sardines because their size rarely exceeds 4 inches. Some Nile perches, over 3.3 feet tall and with jaws decorated with fearsome and impressive teeth, also came to see this curious animal that I was. Soon these majestic fish lost interest in my presence!

While the Nile perch showed a marked disinterestedness towards me, this was not the case with a dreadful reptile that I met during a dive and that froze my blood because the diver is powerless if he wants to attack. This reptile is not the crocodile, but the famous water cobra (*Naja annulata* or *Boulengerina annulata*), feared by all divers because of its lethal bite. This reptile is adapted to underwater life and has a secretive behavior. It is rarely seen and usually lives in rock crevices along the water. From time to time, he swims in open water at shallow depths. However, according to the literature,[29] when the Naja hunts it can dive down to about 33 feet under the surface and stay underwater for about ten minutes. One day as I was going up from a deep dive and was making a decompression stop 16 feet from the surface, I saw a long cylindrical bright brown body with a fairly pale yellow belly. The body was encircled by rings, which are a characteristic of the water cobra. It was roughly 7 feet long and seemed as surprised and frightened as I was. I made sure to remain as long as possible on my decompression level to avoid frightening it. There, 16 feet from the surface with 7 feet between us we remained motionless for a long time. It was watching me; I was watching it. I knew that the Naja normally does not attack unless it feels threatened and, of course, I tried to do nothing that would agitate it. Finally, after a time that seemed endless, my heart beating wildly, it decided it had seen enough of me and quietly left towards a nearby crevice. What an experience!

---

[29] O'Shea, Mark; Halliday, Tim. *Reptiles and Amphibians*.

Tanganyika Lake

The Crocodile, a Constant Danger

I will not speak about Gustave, the Nile crocodile, quoted extensively in the literature,[30] as I have not had the honor to meet him. I will, however, give three case histories illustrating that the crocodile is a ferocious carnivore and a constant danger.

A Morbid Discovery

---

[30] It is the subject of the film *Primeval* directed by Michael Katleman, of the documentary *Le monstre du Tanganyika* (The monster of Tanganyika) broadcasted by France 3, and of the documentary *Capturing the Killer Croc* aired on PBS. Gustave was seen and photographed in 2007. Nobody knows what happened to it.

In the early 1970's, the Government felt that there was overcrowding of crocodiles in Lake Tanganyika. This overcrowding was disrupting the ecological balance and represented a continuing danger for the people who used to come into the lake to wash clothes. The government had therefore allowed the veterinarian Dr. Richard, manager of the veterinary center of Bujumbura and a great crocodile hunter, to eliminate a set number of crocodiles every year. At night Dr. Richard, also a friend of mine, would leave on his inflatable boat and go in the mouth of the Ruzizi River to search for crocodiles, especially numerous along the banks. Dr. Richard was a fearless man and borderline reckless. Once he spotted a prey and thought it was hard to get closer to it by boat, he would not hesitate to get in the water leaving his inflatable boat, too cumbersome and too visible, under the supervision of his few Burundian collaborators. One morning, upon returning from his hunt, he called Hector, a mutual friend with whom we went hunting in Kirundo, to come witness the butchering of a crocodile he had taken home and placed in the backyard of his house. Hector told me what he saw. The reptile was roughly 13 feet long and weighed an estimated 1,500 pounds. It was lying on its back with its belly exposed, significantly bloated. Dr. Richard opened it and, as in horror movies, an entire leg appeared severed at the level of the groin. This was obviously an African woman whose leg had been severed when caught while washing her clothes in the lake. The powerful jaws of crocodiles do not allow lateral jaw movements, and preys or severed limbs are swallowed completely and digested slowly.

Fatality

People were generally taking advantage of the weekend to relax either on the beautiful sandy beaches that border the road leading to Uvira in the former Zaire, or by taking boat trips to visit the many coves along Rumongue Road heading south to Tanzania, or also by going to rest on some sandbanks located near the coast. On a Sunday, a couple that we knew took their speedboat with their two children aged eight and ten years in the direction of one of these delightful beaches. Once arrived, they cast anchor about 33 feet from the beach in a water depth of about 20 inches. The son jumped into the water followed a moment later by his sister. Suddenly the drama erupted. His sister and his parents barely saw a big stir in the water and then nothing. The son was gone! Immediately, they started the engine of the speedboat and circled within the creek for more than five hours. In vain, there was no trace of their son. The darkness fell and they returned to Bujumbura. They resumed their search on the following day and then on the next. It is only on the third day that they discovered, horrified, the body of their son. It was floating in the water barely marked by the teeth that were unquestionably those of a crocodile. Indeed, the crocodile is an opportunistic predator and anything that crosses it, hungry or not, is likely to be caught. This behavior allows the crocodile to build its reserves of food. It usually buried its prey for three to four days in a hole or crevice where it leaves it to decay for some time. The crocodile can return a few days after catching its prey to eat it. In this tragic accident, the crocodile had actually drowned and buried its prey. This one, not secured enough, became loose and floated to the surface.

The crocodile, a constant danger

A Miracle

The third incident reported to us ended in a miracle. A couple had gone to picnic on a fairly wide sandbar located about 300 feet offshore. Once near the sandbar they pulled their boats on it and the whole family came down. Among them was a two-year old child. While the picnic was set, the toddler was playing quietly on the sand roughly 40 feet away from the water under the supervision of his parents. Suddenly panic: a crocodile had slowly and surreptitiously come out of the water and was approaching the child. While the crocodile hunts from a hide in shallow water where it is on the lookout, on land it is dreadful by its speed and the element of surprise, which are the main features of its attacks. Apparently motionless, it is faster than lightning when it leaps upon its prey.[31] In a few seconds and before the crocodile started galloping, the father had the time to grasp his toddler and the family took refuge in the boat. The crocodile dove back into its natural environment and the family got off to a huge fright.

---

[31] The crocodile trots and can gallop for short distances at a speed of about 11 mph. It swims at nearly 19 mph and an adult can even catapult out of the water at a speed of 43 mph.

In the Land of Joys and Sorrows

IX - THE GENOCIDE OF 1972

The Context

The fall of the monarchy occurred on November 28, 1966, and was followed by the establishment of republican institutions structured in a single-party and militarized oligarchy. This context allowed the Tutsi extremists to radicalize their policy of discrimination in its various aspects and adopt a sectarian policy to subjugate the vast Hutu majority. The claims of the latter were always perceived as an abuse of power and were sometimes quelled in blood. Many arbitrary arrests and disappearances reflect the transgression of human rights and the lack of democracy. The rise of the violence, which will become daily in Burundi until the end of the civil war in 2006 and which unfortunately remains today, has been particularly favored by the intolerance and the lack of democracy.

The Massacre of Hutus

No other event can discredit more the first republic than the massacre of the Hutu community that occurred between May and July of 1972.[32] This genocide has its roots in outbreaks of violence and killings of Tutsi by Hutu extremists in the south. On April 29, 1972, an insurrection led by the Hutu members of the police force began in the cities of Rumonge and Nyanza-Lac near the Tanzanian border. According to numerous eyewitnesses, the Hutus engaged in massacres of extreme violence and systematically exterminated all Tutsis and even moderate Hutus. It is estimated that in this brief uprising about 2,000 to 3,000 people were killed before President Micombero declared martial law, reinstated the curfew from 6 p.m. to dawn and began the organized and systematic Hutu massacre targeting the elites, the educated ones, the academics

---

[32] See also *Memorandum sur les massacres répétitifs des Hutu au Burundi* (Memorandum on repetitive massacres of Hutu in Burundi) by the Movement for Peace and Democracy (MPD).

and the military personnel. A friend of mine, a professor at the University of Bujumbura, even witnessed arrests targeting Hutu students attending classes.

When this bloody and ruthless repression, clearly orchestrated and perpetrated by the army, was about to be completed the Tutsi-controlled army then proceeded to the eliminations within the Hutu population, along with the arrests and the massacre of all the Hutu students aged 12 to 18 years. The aim of the Tutsi government was clear and cynical: the near-total elimination of an entire layer of the educated class of Hutu and of Hutu receiving education. This would allow the Tutsi minority to continue ruling over the country unchallenged. It is this particular "ethnic" cleansing of schools that led observers at the time, such as Lemarchand (1996),[33] to speak of genocide, or more exactly of "selective genocide." The carnage wiped out about 5% of the Hutu community within three months. In other words, 200,000[34] to 300,000[35] Hutus were killed or had disappeared during the Tutsi repression. It is also estimated that approximately 500,000 Hutus fled to the former Zaire, Rwanda and Tanzania where large refugee camps were established.

During these troubled times, the nights of Bujumbura, usually so quiet during the curfew imposed by the government, were subject to heavy traffic of trucks of all types, including some military trucks and many private ones. What a strange and unusual motorized choreography many eyewitnesses, including myself have had the sad opportunity of seeing. Eventually, people began to talk about the origin of these private trucks. Most were from traders of Pakistani origin whose trucks, which were normally used to transport coffee, had been requisitioned by the army. As for the content of these trucks, all assumptions went loose but no one really knew for sure.
One day, however, I left the house earlier than usual to go to my research station. I had many rice-growing observations to make and wanted to start this work at dawn. It was 5 a.m. and the curfew had been lifted. I took the road to the airport, which is also the national highway leading to the border of Zaire. I did not make a left turn to go to the airport and continued on the main road for a

---

[33] Lemarchand, René. *Burundi Ethnic Conflict and Genocide.*
[34] Estimate of the United Nations Secretary, General Kurt Waldheim. See also Eggers, Ellen K. *Historical Dictionary of Burundi.*
[35] Estimation from the Hutu opponents.

few miles. Then I turned right on an isolated trail leading directly to the station. I was about 9 miles away from the station when suddenly I saw on my right two dump trucks returning empty from a freshly opened trail where tracks of wide tires and bulldozer chains were highly visible. An odd sight in this place usually so quiet and empty of people and activity. Once the trucks took the road from Bujumbura, curiosity prompted me to explore this trail. I drove about half a mile and then I found a sight I will never forget as it lifted the veil on the fate of all these missing persons. I discovered what I thought was the final resting place of many of these deaths. It was more than likely mass graves where the bodies of countless human beings had been "buried" without any regard. Bulldozers had dug huge pits that had no reason to be in a place so remote. Some pits were covered with fresh earth while others were open and ready to be used. The smell that emanated from these pits left little doubt as to their use. These were mass graves, which corroborates the observations of Jean-Pierre Chrétien and Jean-François Dupaquier "who noticed that the authorities at all levels managed mass graves."[36] The following days I also received an indirect confirmation of my observations. Indeed, during subsequent visits, I found that the open pits had been closed while others had been dug. There was no more room for doubt; the authorities were indeed managing the graves. Moreover, when I think of these graves, I cannot help but think of all those names that have no faces.

I Listen to My Conscience

June 1972. Every morning since I was managing the Imbo Research Station, I was leaving my house around 6 a.m. with my company car Renault R4, picked up my agronomist Nicolas who was waiting at the corner of the former royal palace, and together, we would travel to the station. One morning in June, I went to pick up Nicolas at the usual place. He appeared clearly distraught. He got into the car and told me that soldiers came looking for him at his house around 3.am. He was, however, able to jump at the last moment through the window. Indeed, he was sleeping all dressed up due to the frequent raids made by the army. Since 3 a.m., he had been wandering in the neighborhood. He added that

---

[36] Chrétien, Jean-Pierre ; Dupaquier, Jean-François. *Burundi 1972, au bord des génocides.* (Burundi 1972, on the verge of genocide).

he could not return home because the soldiers would kill him if they found him as they did with all Hutu elites. Indeed, Nicolas was Hutu. He asked me to help him escape. He suggested I take him to the nearby Zootechnical Ruzizi Station, which I was managing for about two months while the Director was on leave. The station was located about nine miles from the Imbo Station along the Ruzizi River, which marks the boundary between Burundi and Zaire. He told me to give him any job for the day, and then his destiny will be in his hands. I understood immediately that he would take this opportunity to try to cross the Ruzizi River and reach Zaire. I knew this crossing was possible but not without risk since the river was not only infested with crocodiles, but the army was doing regular patrols. I started the car and did not hesitate one second to make my decision. I told him I would do everything I could to save him, knowing the consequences of being discovered if I had assisted a Hutu wanted by the military to flee Burundi. I was putting my life in danger and, at best, I could go to jail or be immediately expelled from the country. Another key issue I was confronted with is that Nicolas was totally unknown to the workers of the station. As I drove, I thought about the strategy that I would take to avoid all suspicions when I would introduce Nicolas with the staff and workers of the station. Ideas were racing through my mind and time was running out. We drove for half an hour and I turned on a small sandy trail leading to the Zootechnical Station. At that moment there were a few more miles left to go. I had made my strategy and shared it with Nicolas so that he would not be surprised when we would be in front of the workers. Once at the station, we got out of the car and I introduced Nicolas to the station chief and his team. Then as naturally as possible but with the adequate tone, I told Nicolas to go in the hangar, pick up the theodolite, a surveying instrument, and some lines of sight, gather a team of ten men and go establish the survey of the perimeter. I added that I counted on him to get the job done by 3 p.m., at which time I would come back to pick him up. Then I got back into my car and drove to the Imbo Station. During the entire day, I did not stop thinking about what I asked Nicolas to do in the morning. Would it allow him to flee to Zaire? My mind was racing and I could not stop asking myself many questions. Would a worker suspect something? If so, would the military be contacted and Nicolas arrested or killed? Moreover, if Nicolas had managed to escape in order to cross the Ruzizi River and reach Zaire, could I be suspected of something when I would show up later in the afternoon at the station? I had to be prepared for any possibility.

I returned to the station around 3 p.m. and asked about the progress of the work in the most natural way. To my surprise, a team leader told me that the work had not been completed because "Mr. Nicolas had disappeared during the midday break." I pretended to be irritated by this incident, asking several questions relating to the disappearance of Nicolas. Then, noting that no one seemed to know what really happened I drove back to Bujumbura. There, I announced the disappearance of Nicolas to my management and then went to the police station to make a statement to make things as transparent as possible. I actually spent a good hour at the police station and came away with the promise that this troublesome case would be investigated. Indeed, a police officer came to visit the site a few days after the vanishing of Nicolas, asked many questions to the workers who participated in the topographic survey, then said he would continue the investigation in an attempt to elucidate the fate of Nicolas. During the months that followed his disappearance until the end of my stay in Burundi, the whereabouts of Nicolas remained unknown. Of course, I kept asking myself many questions about the destiny of Nicolas. These questions have remained unanswered for seven long years until 1979 when I returned to Bujumbura as part of consultancy work. It was during this visit that I learned the truth about the circumstances of Nicolas's disappearance and his fate, as I will mention later.

In the Land of Joys and Sorrows

X. POST GENOCIDE

The Duty to Remember

This period, which I call post genocide, also marked the end of our expatriation in Burundi, which we left permanently in September 1974. When the genocide was about to be completed in August 1972, there was only one Hutu nurse left in the whole country and only a thousand Hutu secondary school students who survived the massacre.[37,38] In December 1972, the U.S. Agency for International Development (USAID) actually concluded that "in human terms, Burundi was the worst disaster to occur in 1972."[39]

The genocide of 1972 and the massacres of 1965 received little attention from the media but they left a permanent mark in my memory, in the collective memory of the Hutu population in Burundi and in that of neighboring countries, particularly in Rwanda. The increased tension between Burundi and Rwanda led to numerous border incidents caused by infiltration of Hutu extremists from Rwanda and the punitive massacres made by the Burundian army. These episodes radicalized some individuals of the Hutu population in Rwanda put under pressure by Tutsi activists, known as the R.P.F. or Rwandan Patriotic Front. The 1994 genocide by Hutus in Rwanda that caused the death of nearly 800,000 people according to the United Nations was probably the result of this radicalization.

In 1993, shortly before the Rwandan genocide, civil war broke out in Burundi. It lasted over twelve years. The war that ravaged the country has been the subject of numerous publications.[40]

---

[37] Eggers, Ellen K. *Op. cit.*
[38] Emerson, R. 1975. 'The Faith of Human Rights in the Third World'. *World Politics*. Vol. 27. No. 2. pp.201-226.
[39] Eggers, Ellen K. *Op. cit.*
[40] See particularly the work of Prunier, 1994, Reyntjens, 1995, Lemarchand, 1996 and Ndkimumana, 2005.

Therefore, I will not cover this terrible tragedy except to mention that it led to some 300,000 dead and more than 500,000 refugees in almost total international indifference. Unfortunately, Burundi has little valuable resources and reserves of gas or oil. Therefore, it does not interest rich countries and does not warrant interference from them, as was the case during the recent interventions in highly strategic countries. The book by U.S. Ambassador Robert Krueger and his wife[41] offers a poignant account of the genocide that took place in Burundi. At the risk of his life, Robert Krueger had the merit of revealing the truth to the international community by having graves opened and by interviewing survivors.

Peter Uvin's book[42] is also of particular interest because it complements the traditional justifications of this civil war that focuses on the elite national competition for political power and benefits associated with it. The additional information from Peter Uvin includes the dynamics of radicalization and de-radicalization, the role of elites in the spread of violence, the role of insecurity and injustice or grievance felt by the population. I would like to add to this analysis a complementary aspect, which is very important to me. I will call it the "lasting psychosocial consequences of individual or collective trauma." Indeed, during my eleven years in Burundi and the missions that I made afterwards, I had the opportunity to familiarize myself with the life of the essentially Hutu rural population and better understand the issues and feelings of these people. I gathered this information not via structured interviews, but by a long process of building mutual trust leading to dialogue. During this dialogue, I had no specific questions. My goal was to get my contacts to open up and confide in me. I interacted with men, women, children and the elderly. I discussed with them in front of their *rugo*, the Burundian traditional house, or inside of the latter, in their fields, in the markets or in the plantations.

This is how the lasting psychosocial consequences of the experienced trauma appeared to me as a driving force that gradually developed after the 1965 reprisals and peaked after the 1972 genocide. These psychosocial consequences are associated with the *duty to remember*[43] instilled, especially in children. How

---

[41] Krueger, Ambassador Robert; Tobin Krueger, Kathleen. *From Bloodshed to Hope in Burundi. Our Embassy Years during Genocide.*
[42] Uvin, Peter. *Life after Violence. A People's Story of Burundi.*

many times have I heard during my visits parents telling their children and relatives that we should not bury the memory of suffering and trauma in the past, that we should not forget the victims and the abuses incurred? What I heard during my visits was confirmed in Tracy Kidder's book when Deo, a Rwandan Tutsi whose life is the subject of the book, answers the question posed by the author: "When I asked him how long he thought it would take the Hutus and Tutsis to forget, he said: it will probably take the time that the earth has left."[44]

One difficulty with this *duty to remember* is linked with the fact that victims of serious acts often have at first, or even for a lifetime, difficulties talking about their experiences, while the trauma does not really go away or have lasting psychosocial consequences. The philosopher, Paul Ricoeur, effectively defines the *duty to remember* as a "required memory," a kind of "injunction to remember," which can only be understood in relation with "the horrific events" to which it refers and which has meaning only in relation "to the difficulty experienced by the national community, or by the wounded parties of the political body, to remember these events more peacefully."[45] According to me, the difficulty to remember the events suffered is one element explaining first the selective genocide of 1972, which followed a long period of instability after the events of 1965, and second the civil war that began in 1993. Indeed, how can a family or a collectivity remember more serenely that a whole age group of the Hutu population and almost all its elite has been massacred in 1972? It seems that historians acknowledge the necessity to remember while warning against the abuse of an "injunction to remember."

Yet life has returned to normal when the genocide stopped in late August 1972. However, this life felt rather artificial to me. Indeed the events of 1965, the loss of my entire Burundian staff, the 1972 genocide and the mass graves were still omnipresent in my mind. If my dialogue with the Burundian community has been incredibly

---

[43] The concept or the expression of the *duty to remember*, as it appeared in France in the early 1990s, refers to a moral duty assigned to states to uphold the memory of the suffering in the past by certain population groups. Compared to the tradition of public law and war, it opposes the amnesty that requires forgetting for the sake of appeasement.
[44] Kidder, Tracy. *Strength in What Remains: A Journey of Remembrance and Forgiveness.*
[45] Ricœur, Paul. *La mémoire, l'histoire, l'oubli.* [Memory, History, Forgetting].

rich, the one I had with the expatriate community has been mostly sterile. Indeed, few expatriates have realized except through a well-controlled press or through hearsays the magnitude of what had happened and the potential consequences of these events. Additionally, few cared for it because for many of them there was a partitioning, intended or not, between their lives and those of the Burundian people. Curfew or no curfew, life, parties, picnics on the shores of Lake Tanganyika, and sports activities quickly gained the upper hand.

The Philanthropic Club and the Traffic Lights

September 1972. There was a very active philanthropic club in Burundi known for its charitable and sporting organizations. It decided, however, to diversify its activities. Thus, it proposed to the town of Bujumbura to fund the installation of traffic signals at the intersection of Pierre Ngendandumwe Street and Patrice Lumumba Boulevard. [46] The mayor found the idea original and progressive because Bujumbura had no traffic lights. The permission was given and the work began in earnest, accompanied by an intense campaign of sensitization, which was quite necessary for this innovative type of work. Three months after the work started, the authorities proceeded with great pomp at the inauguration of the traffic lights. In fact, these lights solved strictly nothing and on the contrary slowed the traffic down! If the traffic on Patrice Lumumba Boulevard was relatively dense in the day, this was not the case for Pierre Ngendandumwe Street, where we lived and where Prince Rwagasore Clinic was located. During the night, this street was also virtually deserted. Therefore, there was no need to be a soothsayer to predict that, given the notorious indiscipline of drivers in Bujumbura and the novelty of the traffic lights, some drivers would not lend much attention to these lights. And the inevitable accident happened, but sooner than one could have expected. Less than 24 hours after the inauguration, around 11 p.m., a vehicle ignored the red light while another vehicle was driving down Peter Ngendandumwe Street that was generally deserted at this hour. The shock was terrible and the two drivers did not even benefit from the proximity of the hospital located about 650 feet before this famous intersection because they died

---

[46] Current names.

instantly. This accident put an early end to the traffic light experiment that was for a day the pride of the city of Bujumbura. During my recent visit to Burundi described later in this book, I also noticed that the members of the philanthropic club had genuine common sense. Indeed, after the short and disastrous traffic light experiment, they became more pragmatic and made donations to the town of Bujumbura for conventional stop signs. These signs can be found at several intersections in Bujumbura. Fortunately, wisdom prevailed and these signals were placed at two of the four corners of the intersections and not on all four corners, as is often the case in the U.S.A. While in the U.S.A., road discipline is strictly observed and drivers wait wisely to pass through after a clear stop at the signal; such a concept is obviously inapplicable in Burundi.

President Micombero, a Foosball Game Passionate

October 1972. Nadine and I were quietly having dinner at the restaurant of the Entente Sportive. It was 11 p.m. Suddenly, the manager came to me and said that there was an important phone call for me. I got up and went to the counter to take the call. At the other end, our friend and neighbor Christian told me to join him immediately at his house because he absolutely needed a fourth person to play a foosball game with President Micombero! He warned me to avoid at all costs going through the hedge separating the two houses, which we used to do when we visited one another especially during curfew times, because there were soldiers in the yard and they might shoot me! Really lovely as an invitation! My first reaction was to think this was a joke because Christian was one of those people frequently cracking jokes and was always able to tell jokes for hours. However, I knew that Christian and the President were good friends and loved to drink together, a dedicated habit of the President, and decided to go to this strange appointment. I brought Nadine back home and then walked towards the main entrance of Christian's yard. Soldiers stood guard at the entrance, which confirmed that the invitation was not at all a joke. After having questioned me, they let me enter. The show that I discovered left me speechless. An armored car, headlights on, was parked in the driveway while soldiers guarded the driveway and the surroundings of the yard. Luckily, my friend had warned me not to go through our adjoining fence! I walked down the alley, was greeted by my friend, and then introduced to the President. The latter was already fairly drunk and told me he had heard that I was an avid foosball game player. I replied modestly that I enjoyed this game very much, that I had practiced it a lot when I was a student and that I was of course ready to be the fourth player. In fact, when I was a student I actually played a lot in Brussels' teams and was a good quality Belgian junior. It was 1 a.m. when we started playing and I realized soon that the level of the President and of his partner was not one of the best. Under the effect of alcohol, which the President deeply savored, the quality of their game dropped considerably over time. Three hours later, the President's team did not win once! Taking advantage of a break, my friend then diplomatically suggested reducing somewhat the pace to let the President win! We executed this strategy to perfection and the President left at around 5 a.m. happy with his brilliant performance!

The Driver without a Vehicle

November 1972. A former truck driver had a very serious car accident a few years before and suffered significant brain damage from his accident. On the other hand, all his motor skills were intact and he kept precise memories of driving. He was known by all in Bujumbura and was "driving" a fictional truck in the city's main arteries. He "drove" perfectly within the traffic flow, holding the wheel with both hands, marking the changes of speed, stopping at major intersections and signaling with his arm when he was about to turn left or right. He was also often seen discussing with an assistant driver who was as fictitious as his truck. Indeed, truck and bus drivers in Burundi have an assistant driver responsible for all tasks unrelated to driving. He "drove" for several years without accident. One day, however, turning left, he was hit by a distracted driver and died instantly. Bujumbura had lost its driver fetish. His imaginary truck would never again drive through the city of Bujumbura. A very large crowd gave its sympathy by attending his funeral organized with the assistance of the city.

My Passion for Rugby

December 1972. I used to play rugby when I was attending college and since our relocation in Bujumbura, I joined the Bujumbura team and started playing again. Every Saturday our team was training or playing a friendly match against a local team or one from Zaire or Rwanda. Every Saturday there would be injuries, fortunately light, because the opposing teams, as well as ours, were often composed of inexperienced players who were the source of many mistakes. I remember Nadine continually telling me that this sport was heresy! Then my turn came one afternoon in December 1972. I remember vividly the serious accident of which I was a victim. An awkward adversary was trying to hit the ball and missed it. On the other hand, he did not miss my leg and his straight kick shattered my tibia and fibula. I can still hear the crushing noise like that of a dead branch when the bones broke. I found myself on the ground with the lower part of my leg hanging pitifully at a right angle from the upper part of my leg. I was transported on a man's back because there was naturally no stretcher and was placed in the back of a van. This is how I made the trip from the field to Rwagasore Clinic, not far from home. Nadine had been warned that I had been taken to the hospital and the surgeon, the only one in Bujumbura, arrived an hour after the accident. He decided not to operate immediately because the double fracture was fortunately not open. He reduced the fractures and then put the leg in a cast going up to the upper thigh. The next day I could go home, lying down on a gurney with instructions to limit my movements to a minimum for a period of fifteen days to allow the calcification process to occur without bone movement. Two weeks after the accident, control radiography was made and left no doubts. The bones had moved and the surgery was inevitable. While we trusted the surgeon, we were not as confident about the hygiene and sterilization conditions within the hospital and about the postoperative care. The risk of infection was therefore elevated. A man of my age had indeed a similar accident two years before. He underwent surgery to place a pin in the tibia and, following the procedure, he developed a bone infection that was extremely difficult to cure. The unfortunate underwent five operations in two years and kept serious sequel. Despite assurances from the surgeon we knew well and despite my futile protests, Nadine took the wise decision to send me back immediately to Belgium so that I could be operated under optimal conditions. The day before I left Bujumbura, anxious to resume work as soon as possible, I asked my director to purchase a back seat for my R4 Renault van service. This would allow me to be driven to my workplace in the Imbo Station upon my return. Then I flew to Brussels, with a cast from foot to upper hip. My trip was far from being easy, as it is difficult to cram a straight leg in economy class. On the other hand, the humorous side of this trip still makes me smile. Indeed, I challenge anyone to use an airplane toilet with a whole leg in a cast. Consequently, a flight attendant watched over the corridor when necessary!

January 1973. When I arrived in Brussels, my in-laws greeted me and I spent my first week visiting three surgeons who gave me three different opinions! The first favored complete immobilization for a period of two to three months after reduction of the fracture without operation. The other two favored surgery, each having a different approach. I was faced with a Cornelian dilemma and would rather have preferred not having to choose. I dismissed the first option because I had to return to Burundi as soon as possible if I did not want to lose my job due to an extended absence. Therefore, I opted for the operation at a university hospital where a well-known surgeon practiced and who had been highly recommended. The procedure went smoothly and a consolidation plate and pins were set in place. I still have them and they manifest themselves now and then, according to the sensitivity of metal detectors in airports. Fifteen days later, I received the green light to go back to Burundi.

My Return to Burundi

January 1973. When I returned to Bujumbura and resumed my work, I quickly noticed that it was not easy to come in or go out of the back of my R4. It was even less obvious to move on crutches in the station with temperatures often reaching 100 °F and especially walking on the bunds of rice fields under water, irregular bunds whose width did not exceed 25 inches. I could not afford a fall but I had no choice. Soon, I became an expert in the manipulation of crutches in rice fields to the astonishment of my workers. Upon returning home at night, I would obviously be worn out. The only thing I was looking forward to was to lie down on my gurney and be motionless. I was counting the days because the surgeon in Brussels told me that after two months, my cast could normally be removed and my rehab could start. Yet, things did not turn out well. Indeed, fifteen days after returning from Brussels, the surgeon immediately noticed on the first visit that my ankle had not been re-set back to the correct position when the plaster cast was put on. He told me that if my foot was not set back into the normal position, I would limp for life. After removing my cast, the surgical realignment was carried out, but it significantly delayed the calcification process. Therefore, I stayed four months in a cast before starting physical therapy. I also remember that Africans often looked at me with a sneer and, while laughing, they pointed at me and nicknamed me *mzungu maskini,* which means poor white or handicapped white in Swahili. The word *maskini* is also used frequently by whites and blacks to describe the cohort of handicapped beggars clustered at popular locations, such as the post office or the department stores in town. Then a white moving on crutches in the image of those poor unfortunates was well worth the jeers!

Mzungu Maskini

My Hunt in the Mosso Plain

The Mosso Plain is a major topographical depression which extends over a length of about 186 miles along the southeastern border of the country and which starts at Lake Tanganyika. It is an area of medium altitude ranging between 3,280 and 4,920 feet. It is lined with slopes shattered by deep faults and marked with a large number of depressions that are regularly flooded during pluvial periods. The fauna used to be particularly rich and abounded in elephants, antelopes, common elands, and huge herds of buffalo. For hunters, the Mosso Plain was therefore a very popular place. As for the vegetation, it consisted of wooded savannahs, forest galleries and many swamps with papyrus whose height could reach 10 to 13 feet, harboring numerous snakes. This rather inhospitable setting was the setup of my first and my last big game hunting.

November 1973. A friend asked me if I wanted to accompany him to hunt in the Mosso Plain. Although not a hunter and having no hunting experience, I embarked rather foolishly in this adventure. Indeed, it is not wise to become an improvised large game hunter. Buffaloes and elephants can be extremely dangerous if they feel threatened. In addition, the very least precaution would have been to be properly equipped. This was not the case since my only weapon was a 12 mm gun, which is way too light for this kind of hunting. On the other hand, my friend was a seasoned hunter but he was not better equipped because his large caliber weapon had jammed the day before. From the beginning, we were in a difficult situation. We would have been better off hunting small game than engage into this perilous adventure. Despite many obvious risks, however, we decided to try this crazy adventure. Accompanied by a tracker, we left the passage lodge where we stayed and went off at 3 a.m. to the hunting area. Under the stars that glittered in a sky of astounding purity, we headed toward the marshes and reached them before dawn. At daybreak, the Mosso Plain was imbedded in a fog that dissipated gradually at sunrise. After about three hours of observation and silent progression, we spotted a solitary elephant at about 1,600 feet from our vantage point. In order not to arouse his suspicions, we decided to turn around it while keeping the sun at our back to avoid being blinded and the wind at our front. Indeed, elephants may not have the best eyesight but their hearing and sense of smell are excellent. The slightest rustle is enough to arouse the attention of the animal and the sound of a broken branch makes it uneasy. Its smell reaches perfection and allows it to sniff out the enemy from great distances and no hunter can approach if he moves with the wind at his back. Faced with the elephant, it is the principle of survival in a hostile environment that prevails. We must remember this at any time since unexpected events and dangers are not rare. Experienced in all situations, our tracker had to keep us away from bad surprises so that our hunting would not turn into a bad memory. After two grueling hours of walking in the marshes gorged with water, we were only 800 feet away from this pachyderm. Apparently, it had not detected us. Suddenly, it waved its ears rather significantly, which is a sign of concern. Then, after a mighty roar, it sank into the papyrus swamps and disappeared quickly from sight. However, thanks to our tracker, we managed to find its trail and followed it for more than five hours. The soil of the marsh was patchy and our advance was difficult and exhausting. Often we had water up to mid-thigh and our only horizon was limited to the trail traced by this elephant because the papyruses were up to 13 feet tall and completely blocked our view. Occasionally, we used a high point of the swamp to get a better view, but it was still limited. We advanced in single file, the tracker first, second my friend and me last. Our progress was full of risks because if the animal felt threatened it could face the danger, wait for us and then charge. After five agonizing hours, still no sign of our elephant. Suddenly, I saw the tracker leap to his right, dive into the water and disappear from view. Then, everything happened very quickly. The trail of the elephant, more or less straight until then, was now a sharp right angle. We then cautiously engaged on this ramp and immediately saw the elephant's head about 100 feet away from us. We just had time to see the trump of the animal rise and its ears spread and flap, a sign that the animal felt a presence and imminent danger. Then he trumpeted, dropped his head and charged. I immediately lost sight of it and dove immediately into the water to the left. Time seemed interminable. The earth shook and the noise got closer. I had time to imagine the worst. The elephant passed by a few feet away from me and then the noise faded away. I got up and saw my friend, just as shocked as I was. He told me he had the opportunity to shoot since the animal was so close but did not for fear of not killing the animal instantly, which would have certainly meant our death sentence. Indeed, the wounded and furious animal would certainly have turned around to find the attackers and trample them as other elephants have done in similar circumstances. We were lucky to escape alive from this perilous situation.

Before turning back because the day was about to set, we looked for our tracker, but to no avail. He obviously had abandoned us to our fate. At 3 p.m., we headed off in the opposite direction along the same trail we followed earlier. After more than two hours of backbreaking walk, we were out of the flooded marshes and approached the forest gallery. Another danger was waiting for us.

In a clearing, we suddenly spotted at a distance of about 650 feet a herd of some forty savannah-type African buffaloes that used to spend the hottest hours of the day in the forest galleries. The savannah-type buffalo (Cape buffalo or *Syncerus caffer*), encountered in East Africa and Australia, unlike the forest-type buffalo common in West Africa, is the largest of all buffaloes. Its shoulder height can reach five feet for a weight ranging from 1,450 to 1,750 pounds. While it looks like a peaceful bovine, the Cape buffalo is one of the most dreadful and dangerous animals. Fierce and protective of its territory, the whole herd can charge if threatened. The greatest danger is in fact the unpredictability of the animal. In addition, these buffaloes possess an incredible endurance and a real aggressiveness. They do not fall easily and many guides and hunters are no longer here to talk about it! Therefore, we elected to be wise and cautious. Indeed, the night was falling quickly and it would be suicidal to make a move. We just barely escaped the charge of an elephant we tracked because we had entered its territory. However, the miracle might not occur a second time.

Walking around the clearing, we reached our lodge after a sixteen-hour day of walking. The night already wrapped around the swamps and the forest galleries and gradually the day sounds gave way to those of the deep night. This hunting day was never to be forgotten. Unforgettable because the walk in the marshes full of danger, the sudden encounter with an elephant, followed by that of a buffalo herd has something magical and captivating. However, this day also marked a turning point in my life. It made me aware that the most beautiful hunts are not necessarily those that end with the death of one's adversary. What is so glorious about killing an animal from far away without confronting it? It is as glorious as shooting at a cow in a corridor. I decided to leave all this to others because unfortunately, there are always others who love hunting, who love to kill. This day was my first and last big game hunting and my last hunting for any game.

Our Last Trip to the Virunga National Park

August 1974. We had decided years ago to return to Belgium when the constructions in the Imbo Plain would be completed. This moment had arrived. In June 1974 at the end of the school year, Nadine and Karin returned to Belgium. Eric and I stayed until early

September. This allowed me to pack and ship all our belongings to Belgium. I also wanted to complete some agronomic trials that I had set up. Mid-August, the house was almost empty and Eric and I began the preparations for our last trip outside Burundi. This trip was to take us to the Virunga (volcano in Swahili) National Park, in Zaire. This park, known as the Albert National Park prior to the independence of the Congo in 1960, is located about 12 miles from the border town of Goma in today's Congo. It includes the flanks of a volcanic chain, among which are the active volcanoes Nyamuragira, *the one that commands*, and Nyiragongo, *the one that smokes*. The latter carries its name well. In the day one can see clouds of white smoke escaping from its crater, while at night glowing ash light up the sky. This volcano is famous for having destroyed about 40% of the city of Goma during its eruption in 2002. It is adjacent with the Ruwenzori Mountains National Park[47] in Uganda and the Volcanoes National Park in Rwanda.

For this trip, I had my Fiat 128. This front wheel drive car behaves remarkably in muddy conditions, but suffers from a low ground clearance. I therefore had the body of the car raised and the oil paint protected since we were running the risk of meeting a large number of deep ruts on the roads of the park. Indeed, I had been told that these roads were in pitiful shape due to the lack of maintenance common to all roads in Zaire. The car ready, we headed for the border of Rwanda then for Gisenyi, a town on the north shore of Lake Kivu. Located at an altitude of 4,800 feet, Lake Kivu is the highest in Africa. Its bed sits upon a rift valley that is slowly being pulled apart. This causes significant volcanic activity in the area and makes it particularly deep. Indeed, its depth of 1,575 feet is ranked 15th in the world. It is also unique in that it is one of three lakes in the world containing large amounts of carbon dioxide dissolved in deep waters, the others being lakes Nyos and Monoum in Cameroon.[48] We arrived early evening in Gisenyi and left the next day to cover the five miles between Gisenyi and Goma. The border formalities took place without incident and we took the road towards the Nyiragongo about nine

---

[47] Ptolemy assimilated the Ruwenzori Mountains with the Mountains of the Moon and hypothesized that the Nile had its source there. His *Geography* was the travelling standard until the sixteenth century.

[48] Lake Kivu is also one of the lakes identified with limnic eruptions, together with lakes Monoum and Nyos in Cameroon. In 1986, Lake Nyos has also exploded and released about one cubic kilometer of carbon dioxide, deadly at high concentration, which led to 1746 deaths in a landscape virtually untouched, while over 3,000 people were forced away from their homes and were grouped in camps. (Source Wikipedia)

miles away. At the foot of Nyiragongo is one of the last wildlife sanctuaries in the world with its mountain gorillas made famous by Diana Fossey. [49] As it was forbidden to visit the gorillas with a minor, we traveled the lower parts of the volcano and the park and discovered an extraordinary variety of wild animals, probably one of the largest concentrations in Africa before the start of the civil war in 1997. During our visit, the park still included numerous small tracks leaving the main road. We had no guide, and these secondary tracks were ours only. On the other hand, the deep ruts characterizing these tracks were a real challenge for us because they did not correspond to the spacing of my Fiat's wheels. The latter was snorting a bit on these ruts, bravely going into the mud and in places was forced to fight its way through a tunnel of vegetation. Our speed often felt below 3 mph and I did not dare think about what would have happened if we had stayed mired in the mud or stuck in a rut, because throughout our journey we came across nobody. We were alone among the wild animals including many antelopes, warthogs, buffaloes and majestic elephants. We also stopped to observe these last ones near our vehicle. Eric then got out of car to get as near as 100 feet from them. The elephants seemed intrigued by this little person approaching them and their ears moved continuously, reflecting some nervousness. Yet, they seemed so quiet and so peaceful that it never crossed my mind that they could charge. We enjoyed an extraordinary spectacle, unbelievable, and, I must admit, very daring and dangerous. It would be impossible to repeat today because of the requirement to be guided and accompanied. We took advantage of the park like no other, and it offered us an experience much closer to the wilderness of the bush and the jungle with the excitement and danger that they entail.

---

[49] American zoologist renowned for her study of the life of gorillas in Rwanda covering a period of 18 years. She was murdered in 1985 and her murder remains unsolved.

Post Genocide

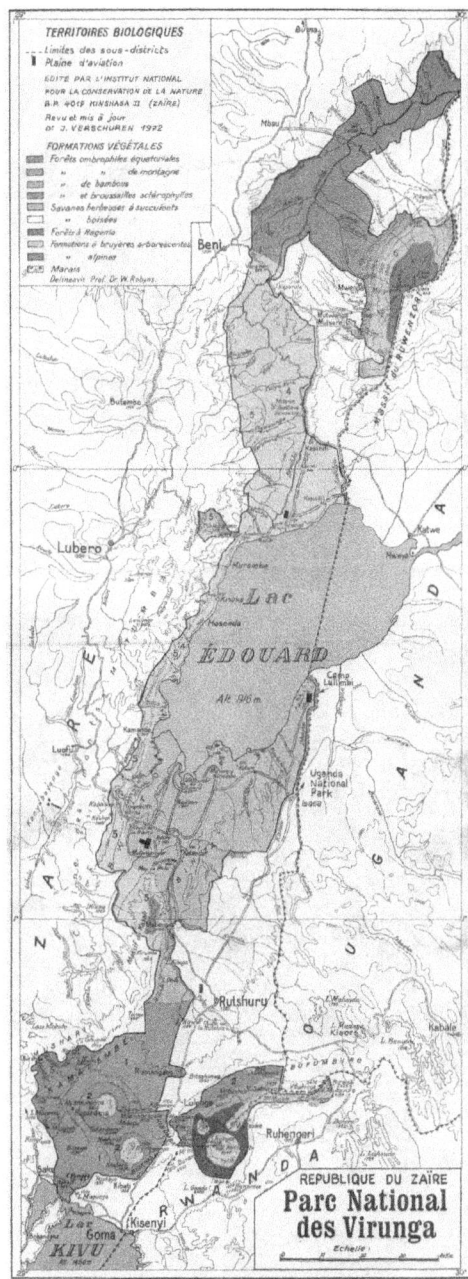

Virunga National Park

143

In the Land of Joys and Sorrows

Crossing a river by ferry

A trail in the park

Eric and the elephants

We then continued our slow progress toward the hotel of Rwindi, located about a three hours drive from Goma. It is there that we had the incredible opportunity to meet an extraordinary character, Jean-Pierre Hallet. Mr. Hallet, who passed away in early 2004, was an unusual character recognized internationally for his humanistic qualities. He was a sociologist, an agronomist and an ethnologist. He was a legendary adventurer who lost his right hand by dynamiting fish in Lake Tanganyika to feed a starving population of Mosso Pygmies in Burundi. He is also known for his relentless work, which led for the preservation of life and culture of the Efe Pygmies of the Ituri Forest in contemporary Congo. We stayed with him for a long time, sharing our experiences in tropical agronomy and especially listening to him talk about the extraordinary life he conducted independently. No one else had this knowledge of Africa in general and of the Pygmies in particular. We had the privilege of meeting a man of incredible charisma whose book, *Congo kitabu: a giant amongst pygmies* remains one of my favorites in the field of African life as perceived by an expatriate.

Then we bid farewell to these incomparable landscapes and exuberant wildlife. As we drove back towards Bujumbura, one last surprise awaited us. As we were about to cross the border post of Rwanda separated from that of Burundi by a long bridge over the River Kanyaru, a customs officer got out of his corrugated sheets shelter to inform us that the border was closed to traffic from noon to 2 p.m. and that we needed to wait. According to my watch, it was only 11:30 a.m. What was I to do? Arguing about the time would be useless and could only irritate him. However, I did not give up knowing that things can often be "discussed" in Africa. Therefore, I followed the customs officer as he was returning to his dugout and was surprised to see his colleagues from Rwanda and Burundi busy playing this exciting African board game, called *kisoro* in Swahili or *urubugu* in Kirundi and which is usually played with seeds of the Goldenrain tree. The customs officials then interrupted their game spiced up with Primus, the famous Burundi beer, and questioned me about the purpose of my visit. I followed by asking them if it was possible to put a stamp on our passports and let us through because my son and I were exhausted after a very long trip. One of the Burundian officials told me that the stamp I needed to return to Burundi was unfortunately in their shelter on the other side of the bridge and he did not intend to get there before the opening of the border. With this said, I thought I would have to wait until 2 p.m. To my surprise, however, the official added that he understood that we were tired. He explained that he was going to open the gate and that all I had to do was to go in their shelter and stamp our passports. I could not believe it! I offered them some beers, crossed the bridge and put the appropriate stamps on our passports before returning to Burundi. This story crowned our exquisite trip with humor. Ten days later, we took the plane for Belgium and for a new phase in life.

XI. A FEW YEARS LATER

A Different Immersion

October 1978. I returned to Burundi for a period of six months as part of a consultancy work. The political context had changed since Micombero's presidency. Overthrown by the coup of November 1, 1976, he disappeared from political life and was replaced by Colonel Bagaza. The latter became President of the Second Republic on November 10, 1976. Micombero spent three years under house arrest in Ngozi in the north before being exiled to Mogadishu in Somalia, where he died in 1983 at the age of 46 under conditions that some find suspicious.

Lake Cyohoha

My mission was located on the southern part of Lake Cyohoha, also known as Lake Cohoha. The latter is situated at an altitude of about 4,400 feet in the northeast of Burundi at about 186 miles from Bujumbura and 12.5 miles from the town of Kirundo. This lake covers an area of 23.2 square miles, extends in Rwanda and is part of a series of seven lakes including Lake Rwihinda. Lake Rwihinda, known as "Lac aux Oiseaux" or Birds' Lake, is renowned as a bird sanctuary and is the only lake in Burundi benefiting from wild life protection.[50] Lake Cohoha presents an uncommon physical beauty. Its shape is elongated and very jagged and is extended by eight long arms and a series of small arms attached to a central corridor. It includes a center island called *akagwa*, and some secondary floating islands called *ibishinga* moving on the lake with the wind. The sides are often high and steep and the bottom hard. This lake is like the end of the world for the people of the capital and this is exactly how I experienced it. At the time, all the roads were dirt roads from the lake to Bugarama, or about 170

---

[50] It is the migratory passage and wintering for about twenty species of birds. These birds come from Europe, arrive at the site in December and return in April.

miles before driving towards Bujumbura on the asphalt road. It would take more than six hours of spicy ruts and jolts to travel the distance separating my cottage situated on the banks of the lake from the capital.

I used the budget of the project I was responsible for to rent this cottage located at about 70 feet from the lake and consisting of six small rudimentary bedrooms and one living room. On the outside was located the shower, fed by the water of the lake, and a small generator used several hours at night. The setting was idyllic but life was difficult. Indeed, the consultants who worked with me came only for short periods to perform specific tasks. As the consultants were going back and forth, I often was on my own in this isolated cottage. I was looking at the beautiful sky that sparkled above my head with bright planets adoring both the early evening and predawn sky. I was looking at the moon looming low in the sky above the rippling water of the lake, leaving a long trail of shimmering light on the water surface. I was staring at the planetary jewel that beckoned me as soon as the sky started to darken. However, I felt alone in the middle of this gigantic universe, I felt lonely in this world facing the lake.

Lake Cyohoha

I Hang Around with Hippos

In evening times, in my solitude, some rather large and noisy companions who had the habit to manifest themselves at dusk, frequently visited me. The lake was indeed the habitat of a few hippos. During the day, the hippos spent almost all of their time wallowing in shallow water because their skin needs to be kept wet for a good part of the day to avoid dehydration, as they do not have true sweat glands. Instead of perspiring, however, hippos have specialized pores that ooze an oily pink substance, which creates a layer of mucous that protects hippo skin from sunburn and keeps it moist. In the evenings, after the hot sun has set, hippos come out of the water for a night of grazing in the fields of the natives. A hippo ingests up to 110 pounds of vegetation per day and if there is not enough grass in its path, it can devastate an entire field of vegetable crops in a few hours. To keep them away the peasants would alternately keep watch all night, banging on empty gasoline drums. Despite these precautions, crop damage was unfortunately often considerable. In appearance, they are placid in the water; hippos are, however, feared by most animals, including the Nile crocodile. In Africa, they are responsible for the greatest number of human fatalities. They are particularly dangerous in the evening and at night when they graze on the banks. In such cases, I would recommend not standing between these mammals and the water because hippos, despite their stocky shape and short legs, can easily outrun a human. Estimates of their running speed vary from 18 mph to 25 mph, or even 30 mph. The hippo can maintain these higher speeds for only a few hundred yards.

My swimming fellow

The presence of these voluminous mammals generated major problems for me, since swimming in the lake was part of my daily life. Despite the danger, I swam every day about one mile. I had taken some precautions, though, by posting a guard on the beach to warn me of the possible presence of our aquatic friends. I would carefully and quickly swim away from the coast as fishermen told me that our hippos spend most of the day near the banks and preferred shallow muddy waters. Indeed, hippos are not good swimmers. They take advantage, however, of their specific gravity to sink and walk or run along the bottom of a river or lake. They can remain completely submerged for ten minutes and move around at about 5 mph by pushing off from the bottom of the lake with their toes. It is, therefore, extremely difficult to guess where they will resurface after diving. When the guard spotted hippos, I would wait at about 300 feet from these voluminous companions until they deign move away or dive. In the latter case, I was solely relying on myself, looking for the turmoil in the water that announces their resurfacing. Several times, I had very close calls. Nothing, however, would have prevented me from swimming in this beautiful lake.

And Not Only Hippos

At the end, it was not weeks of swimming with the behemoth hippos that took a heavy toll on my health, but a tiny blood-sucking worm, a nematode of the genus *Schistosoma*, which tend to be 0.4-0.8 inches long. These nematodes, whose intermediate host is a freshwater snail, are responsible for a highly significant parasitic infection of humans by causing the disease bilharzia or schistosomiasis, which is the second world parasitic endemic after malaria with hundreds of millions infected worldwide. I had avoided the hippos but did not escape the blood-sucking worm and its perverse effects. While my long mission ended and I was about to return to Belgium, I felt suddenly feverish and lethargic. A few weeks after my return to Belgium, I developed a high fever accompanied by shivering, cough and muscle pain that required a stay in the tropical hospital in Antwerp, Belgium. The examinations revealed that I was suffering from bilharzia. At that time treatments were essentially based on relatively successful antimony derivatives. However, a new drug, Ambihar or niridazole, had also just been approved. Though the drug was proved to be very toxic to humans, especially for the nervous system and had dangerous side effects, I was given that new drug to control my bilharzia. The side effects were immediately devastating and after one day of treatment, I felt sicker than before the start of the treatment. Moreover, the latter lasted seven days!

My Reunion with Nicolas

June 1979. During this month, I returned to Burundi as part of a consultancy mission for another three months. My base was Bujumbura. One evening, I went to a restaurant located on Lake Tanganyika and sat at the bar before going to dinner. I looked around to see if there was anyone I knew from the time we were living in Burundi. Suddenly, my eyes landed on a familiar face, which I stared at for a long time. The person was sitting sideways from me and it was difficult to identify him with certainty. Yet, he seemed extremely familiar. Suddenly, I became convinced that this was Nicolas, who without my assistance in 1972 would probably no longer be part of this world. I did not hesitate and went up to him. He instantly recognized me and we fell into the arms of each other in front of eyes that could not understand what linked us. Seized by the emotion, we immobilized in the arms of one another. Then we sat at a table safe from eavesdroppers and he told me his extraordinary adventure. After I left him at the Zootechnical Ruzizi Station with specific instructions about the work to be done, he began working with the employees who were to assist him. Everything was proceeding normally. However, it was very difficult, he said, to pretend moving away from the workers so as to try to cross the Ruzizi River and go to Zaire. He had to act very cautiously to avoid alerting the workers. Indeed, they already did not know him and seemed particularly suspicious. This was a normal reaction in a tense atmosphere of witch-hunt. Finally, during the lunch break he had the opportunity to move away from the group. He walked an hour towards the Ruzizi River because he knew there were smugglers facilitating the crossing in exchange of steep financial contribution. After reaching the river, he walked along its bank for more than two hours and finally came across a boat. The deliverance was at hand and half an hour later, he was across the river in Zaire. He was saved facing an uncertain future. He walked into the bushes for five long days towards Bukavu where he lived as a refugee for seven years earning his living with odd jobs. In early 1979, he observed that the political management of Burundian refugees was not on the agenda of the Zairian government and that ethnic tensions between locals and refugees grew by the day. Therefore, he decided to take the calculated risk of returning home. He thought his life would be less exposed than it was in Zaire. He told me that he had lost everything, from his property to his work, and he had not heard from many members of his family. However, life went on and he still kept the hope of a better life.

After two hours of discussion, we parted as brothers. Today, more than thirty years after our last meeting I still think of him and ask myself many questions on the eve of my return trip to Burundi. Was he amongst an estimated 500,000 Burundians who fled Burundi after the start of the civil war in 1993 and found refuge in Tanzania or contemporary Congo? If once more he was a refugee, did he return to Burundi after January 2002 when the first refugees started coming back to their native home with the assistance of the United Nations Refugee Agency? Is he still alive? I doubt that one day I will find answers to these questions. Never however, will I be taken away the bliss of the duty accomplished, that of having contributed to saving a person from death.

The Confrontation of Two Perspectives

End of 1980. I was recruited by the World Bank, in Washington, D.C at the end of the year. During my 21 years of career in rural development within the organization, I had the opportunity to travel the world with focus on selected countries in Francophone Africa, the Indian Ocean and Southeast Asia. While Burundi was not part of my regular responsibilities, I remained deeply attached to this country, which I consider as my second home. How can it be different after living eleven years and carrying out numerous missions afterwards in that country? Therefore, I had placed on one wall of my office a magnificent poster of Burundi showing the famous drummers. I also continued to follow the political and economic developments of the country and went back there for a short and last mission in 1989.

In the mid-1990s, while I had recently been assigned to the Southeast Asian region, the director of that region came to see me in my office. After an update on various issues related to countries I was involved with, my poster drew his attention and he asked me why I had it on my wall. I gave him my reasons referring in particular to the many years spent in Burundi. I continued my explanation by saying that this stay allowed me, in my view, to have gained a certain field experience and to better understand the highly complex human relations between different ethnic groups of that country. I knew of course that the World Bank, which considered the democratic evolution of the country as promising, heavily courted Burundi at that time. I was therefore not surprised when my manager asked me what I thought of the future of Burundi. I told him that despite very positive indicators of economic development and the seriousness shown by the government to begin a process of democratization, I was not particularly optimistic about the future of Burundi. Notably, I mentioned that the contact I had with people during my expatriation and my subsequent visits led me to think that peace had certainly not returned to the countryside. To me it seemed obvious that the memory of the abuse endured by the Hutu and Tutsi people during the genocides of 1965 and 1972, and by Tutsis during the massacres of August 1988 at Ntega and Murangara in the north was far from fading away. Finally, I told him that I did not think that the current improvement and the "sunshine policy" between Burundi and the Bank would continue. My manager did not even take the time to try to understand my arguments and simply replied that I was a pessimist. Before leaving, I could not resist telling him that we indeed had two diametrically opposed views of the future of Burundi, one based on field experience and contacts with the population and the other one based on economic data and government contacts. I concluded by saying that it would certainly have been interesting to discuss these views in more depth, but given the lack of dialogue only the future would tell. Two years after our conversation the civil war erupted in late 1993. This war lasted twelve years and left the country devastated. Subsequently, of course I had many opportunities to see my manager. The argument we had in 1990 about the future of Burundi was, however, never invoked! Of course, I would much prefer that his opinion prevailed, and that the deadly conflict never occurred.

XII. A RETURN TO THE ROOTS

Why This Book

Over the last thirty years, I have had many opportunities to narrate certain aspects of our fascinating life in Burundi, and those no less fascinating of my subsequent visits. Through the stories and questions, other memories came to complement the first ones. This incited me to consolidate them into a narrative of our life and of my subsequent visits in that remote country so dear to my heart.

After my last visit in late 1989, I continued following up closely with the political and economic developments of Burundi, which is, as we have seen, characterized by a long history of violence, coups, assassinations and massacres. July 10, 1993 marked a turning point in the history of Burundi, since Ndadaye became the first democratically elected Hutu President. However, this progress was very short-lived. Three months after taking office, Tutsi extremists assassinated the new President. He is buried on the site of the former royal palace. This tragic event marked the beginning of a civil war, which lasted from 1993 to 2006. During this long period, the fighting between the Tutsi-dominated army and various Hutu rebel movements was disastrous. It led to some 300,000 dead people, mostly civilians, according to the United Nations and the exodus of more than 800,000 refugees or about 10% of the population. This conflict brought ethnic instability in the region, which created the fertile ground for the 1994 genocide in Rwanda and chaos in the neighboring Congo. In addition, the economic situation worsened significantly during the conflict and was aggravated by the embargo, consecutive to the second coup of President Buyoya in 1997.

Throughout the civil war, Burundians lived in constant insecurity, famine invaded the country, drugs were lacking, sugar was in shortage, people lived in displaced persons' camps, school fees became impossible to afford for families with humble incomes, and the average employee could no longer meet his or her monthly obligations. The powers in place did not have the political strength to find a solution to the war going in the country and to the resurgence of scourges like hunger, AIDS, and malaria.

August 19, 2005. This date marks the election of Pierre Nkurunziza as the new President of Burundi. A former rebel son of a Tutsi mother and a Hutu father, he lost his father in the great massacres of Hutus in 1972. He joined the underground after barely escaping an anti-Hutu raid at the University of Bujumbura, also in 1972. Pierre Nkurunziza brought a breath of hope on the region of the Great Lakes. However, some sources suggest that the political climate in Burundi deteriorated immediately after the election of the new government[51,52] The latter arrested those critiquing it, muzzled the press, committed abuses against human rights, and strengthened its control over the economy. Subsequently, Burundi did make substantial progress in the field of democracy and in easing ethnic tensions.[53] In 2009, the peace process was consolidated.[54] On July 8, 2010, the Constitutional Court validated the Presidential election of June 28 of that year, giving the outgoing President, the only candidate to run to succeed himself, a second five-year term. The daunting task awaiting the reelected President included the rebuilding of the socio-economic foundations of the country, which has been devastated by the 1993-2006 civil war that sank over 68% of its population below the poverty line, according to the United Nations.

After the Presidential elections, the political context continued to evolve favorably, according to official sources. Such an encouraging turnout was confirmed by the positive impressions I gathered from acquaintances who visited Burundi for business or pleasure. This reinforced my desire to return to Burundi to complete my book with a personal assessment of the situation. As Nadine was strongly encouraging me to make the trip that I had so much at heart, I initiated all the necessary entry and sanitary requirements to travel to Burundi at the end of 2010. Given the exorbitant prices charged in the United States for vaccinations and prophylactic medications, I managed to complete these requirements while on a short trip in Belgium. Then, I applied for

---

[51] ICG. *Burundi: Democracy and Peace at Risk.*
[52] Swiss Peace. "Burundi's Endangered Transition," FAST Country Risk Profile.
[53] ICG. *Burundi: Finalizing Peace with the FNL.*
[54] ICG. *Burundi: To Integrate the FNL Successfully.*

my visa using the form available on the website of the Embassy of Burundi in Washington, D.C. I went to the embassy and realized it was not easy to enter the premises. Despite my repeated ringing of the bell, no one came to the door, which remained stubbornly closed. I asked an employee who was leaving another embassy located on the same floor if the Embassy of Burundi was open. He replied in the affirmative while mentioning that the bell had not been working for some time and that I had to knock assertively at the door. To my embarrassment, he walked his talk and the door opened. I entered into the embassy while apologizing for the noise and handed my paper. After the passport clerk confirmed that the bell was indeed broken for some time, she went over my visa application. She gave it back immediately and stated to my great astonishment that this was not the correct form. She explained that the form had recently been changed but the form on the website of the embassy, which I used, had not yet been updated! Here I was, immediately back into a very administrative circuit! So I was asked to come back to the embassy with the new visa application duly completed, as well as with additional documents such as a plane reservation, hotel booking and local contacts. I had no problems providing these documents but I still wonder how likely visitors would apply to travel to Burundi without a hotel booked in advance and without local contacts. A final surprise awaited me when I was about to pay for the visa. Indeed, I noticed that the price of the visa was different depending on the nationalities and was twice as expensive for an American citizen than for a Belgian citizen. I could have used my Belgian passport to avoid this extra cost but I chose not to due to lack of time.

Burundi, November 17, 2010. The night was dark and without clouds. The plane started its final approach to the Bujumbura airport where it was about to land within minutes. It was 8 p.m. I was nervous, as if it were a first visit to a country unknown to me. Yet, accustomed to traveling around the world, I never felt this feeling that transcended me. It was a feeling of happiness and curiosity mixed with some anxiety to see this country we loved so much. I was aware, however, that the Burundi I knew had changed after more than twelve years of civil conflict and continuing instability. Going down was lagging and I found myself surprised, yet I should not have been, by the lack of lights over the Burundian countryside throughout the descent. Darkness ruled the country as it has done since the beginning of time. It is only near the airstrip of the airport that I perceived at last the lights of the city of Bujumbura, its beautiful hills overlooking the majestic Lake Tanganyika and the headlights of a few moving cars.

Upon arrival at the airport heavily worn out, a first administrative constraint awaited me. Before proceeding to the passport control, there was an initial check to verify if the very detailed immigration document we had been given in the plane was properly completed. The immigration officer in charge of this task announced that the document we received in the plane was no longer valid and that another one needed to be completed. The story of the embassy was repeating itself! This new document was, as an irate passenger pointed out to immigration officials, identical to the first one except for the color and presentation. I still wonder about the logic of this change that actually adds nothing to the information requested on the previous form. After checking the luggage, I was supposed to be picked up by a taxi from the hotel where I had made my reservation. He shone by his absence and I had to negotiate the fare with another taxi. This negotiation was delayed somewhat because there were three drivers fighting for the potential customer! Finally, I went into a broken-down taxi and we left for the hotel. Throughout the drive, strangely silent due to the virtual absence of traffic, memories ran into my head. I felt at home.

Bujumbura

Upon arriving at the hotel, another surprise awaited me. The receptionist could not find my name on the list of reservations and there was no room available! At around 10 p.m. and after 24 hours of traveling, I was exhausted and really did not want to start searching for a hypothetical hotel. Finally, after further reading of the reservation book, the clerk noticed that I was registered under my first name!

The next day I took a taxi to go to the center of the city about ten minutes away from the hotel. I was shaking with excitement. The taxi dropped me at the beginning of Prince Louis Rwagasore Avenue, which is one of the main streets of Bujumbura. Then, I walked through the city for over four hours and did the same the following days. I had so much to discover or rediscover. I was happy. First, I was amazed to observe the high concentration of people in the city in general, and downtown in particular compared

A return to the Roots

to the pre-war situation. Indeed, the total population of Bujumbura is currently estimated at 400,000 inhabitants, while it was only 200,000 before the war twenty years ago. This demographic explosion is mainly caused by strong migrations from rural areas and it creates a significant increase in the number of beggars, pickpockets and people at loose end. During my walks, some of these robbers actually demonstrated their talented expertise to me. Indeed the first day of my visit, my cell phone was gone as well as the equivalent of 50 U.S. dollars I just changed at the bank. I discovered the theft when, after having my lunch, I wanted to pay and I did not have a penny! This mastery, however, showed its limits during a second attempt. Its author, unfortunately for him, was not caught with his hand in the cookie jar but with his hand in my pocket. He had actually managed to insert three fingers into the pocket of my jeans and was about to steal my second cell phone I just bought. As I was on the alert after what had happened the night before, I felt a very light touch in my pocket, grabbed his hand, twisted his arm and made him fall on the ground. The surrounding crowd was dumbfounded and would not stop chanting, "A thief, a thief!" I kept him on the floor for a long time, then I let him go and he ran under the jeers of all the onlookers. I think this lifter will remember that his job is not without risk. I was also surprised to see that everywhere I looked I was the only white person around. Indeed, twenty years ago it was perfectly normal for white persons to roam around in the city center. However, I learned the following days that safety has become a serious concern in Bujumbura during the daytime and that walking in the streets at night should be avoided. In spite of these concerns, I felt generally safe in the city and found that Bujumbura was still a fun place for a foreigner to roam during the daytime, but that you have to have your wits about you. "Watch out for pickpockets." I also found that unemployment has become a curse that affects all classes of the Burundian society. University graduates are not spared and many people are forced to become taxi drivers or to accept some small jobs, incommensurate with their skills.

Throughout my wandering, I was also surprised by the extremely high density of vehicles of all kinds. Some dilapidated as the majority of the taxis and other means of transport; others included luxury and all-terrain vehicles owned by various embassies, international and bilateral agencies, nongovernmental organizations (NGOs) and funded projects. The number of motorcycles zigzagging between vehicles and the growing number of mototaxis, with their passenger without a helmet, is also part of this wild and heavy traffic. Crossing a busy street as a pedestrian is, therefore, a major and risky challenge. I could observe that the number of accidents is unfortunately quite high because many drivers have little or no driving experience. Indeed, it is easy to obtain a license without knowing how to drive because anything can be bought. In addition, being a passenger on a motorcycle taxi is a guaranteed short-term accident! During my endless walks, I also visited the residential areas and was taken aback when I observed that many homes have lost the warm and welcoming touch they once had. They are now routinely surrounded by brick walls topped with barbed wire obscuring the gardens we had the pleasure to observe and are closed to prying eyes by heavy metal doors, and this since the recent years of civil war.

I was also surprised by the number of new buildings, whether administrative, hotel or residential ones. This development also contrasted with the deterioration of many hotels and recreational buildings. The former Paguidas Hotel, where we stayed when we arrived in Burundi, has become a sordid hotel renamed "Le Doyen" Hotel guarded by zealous employees ensuring that it is not photographed. I was told that prostitutes mostly use his ramshackle rooms. As for the former sports complex, which witnessed many executions during the various coups, only a dilapidated field remains of it. The disfigurement of the city center is just as significant. For example, in Prince Louis Rwagasore Avenue the luxury shops have disappeared in favor of small tasteless shops selling fabrics, various food and especially mobile phones, which have become indispensable in everyday life. Then, among these small businesses, I was struck to see a poster with President Obama, who is very popular and revered in Burundi. As for the former royal palace, which reminded me like it was yesterday the time when the fate of my former agronomist Nicolas had shifted from an inescapable death to freedom, it had been totally ransacked during the civil war and unfortunately, only ruins are left of it. Then, continuing towards the hills overlooking the city, I discovered a completely new neighborhood of luxury homes built up, unfortunately without much urban constraints. They belong mostly to officials or former officials of the state. According to what I heard, there is, however, a general understanding that only corruption made these buildings possible. Indeed, since a minister earns about four hundred U.S. dollars per month and a general manager about two hundred dollars, it is easy to deduce that all these new buildings are linked to the scourge of corruption. Further south of the city along the lake, new buildings have also emerged from the ground. They also abide by little urban constraints and leave the new owners at the mercy of any flood from the lake at the image of the one that caused so much damage in that area in the 1970s. However, along the lake towards the Congolese border, I was pleasantly surprised to find that some sandy beaches were beautifully developed and are now offering opportunities for dining and water activities.

Avenue Prince Louis Rwagasore "Obama Shop"

The former Hotel Paguidas

The former Sports Complex

Finally, the change that shocked me most is that of the militarization of the state. At the end of the civil war in 2006, the government committed to a gradual reintegration of many armed rebels into the military, the traffic police and various private protection systems. Parts of them, considered less suitable, have not been reinstated and they returned to the bush often with their arms through a modest financial compensation. Therefore, the number of men in various uniforms and armed with automatic weapons is impressive, but the discipline and poise of these bearers of weapons have left me wary. I also noticed that drivers are subject to frequent and often arbitrary checks by corrupted armed forces asking for money either for imaginary infractions or for true infractions instead of delivering a ticket because their meager income of eighty U.S. dollars per month for a corporal is insufficient to make ends meet. As seen in the following chapter, corruption has reached unimaginable levels.

The Problem of Corruption

Corruption exists in all spheres of social life. Nobody is immune from this scourge. All contracts are affected including short or medium term leases for houses, apartments or other buildings, which have no value and may be terminated at any time by a short notice if the owner finds a higher bidder. This problem is best illustrated by the 2009 termination of the thirty-year contract awarded to the Yacht Club of Bujumbura whose tenants had a month to move. The Circle is now located at the "Petit Bassin" along the northern shore of the lake. As for the building of the old circle, despite the promises of rehabilitation made by its new owner, it is totally abandoned. Increases in rents without notice are equally frequent using added value of the house as an excuse even though it is the tenant who paid the price of renovation or alteration with the consent of the owner, of course! Arbitrariness is king and money is law. While corruption appeared to be relatively subdued before the outbreak of civil war in 1993, the dysfunction of the state in consecutive disruption of authority has been a fertile ground for the development of corruption. Burundi is also found among the eight countries perceived as most corrupted in the world since it ranks 170 out of 178 countries in the latest rankings of Transparency International with a score of 1.8 out of 10.[55] I actually witnessed within a single day and then at the airport upon my return that corruption does affect all sectors. First, a police officer stopped my taxi because I was not wearing a belt. I agreed to pay the fine, which amounted to seven U.S. dollars, provided I would get a receipt against my payment. As the police officer pretended not to have tickets with him, he came into the cab to continue our discussion. Given my insistence to obtain this receipt, he quickly changed his tactic and asked me for two beers. Since I

---

[55] Transparency International. 2010 Corruption Index.

had little time to discuss further, I paid him his beer for which he warmly thanked! The same evening, in a large hotel in Bujumbura, the butler suggested me the buffet for dinner. It was attractive and reasonably priced and I placed my order. Knowing that credit cards are not accepted in most hotels, or restaurants and shops--which does not make life easier--I paid the bill in cash and asked for a receipt. He apologized and told me that unfortunately, he had given the last receipt from his book but I could come back the next day if I wanted! I leave you to draw the conclusion! Then leaving the same hotel, I noticed that there were no taxis. Realizing what I was looking for, the driver of a luxury limousine owned by a foreign delegation dining at the hotel offered to bring me back to my hotel for the fare of a normal taxi. "I am inheriting a luxurious taxi," I said jokingly. He laughed and drove me back to my hotel! Finally, upon my departure, at the airport of Bujumbura, an immigration officer asked me shamelessly to give him the Burundian francs I had left! I explained that I had given my last bills to the taxi driver who had accompanied me throughout my stay. Not at all confused by my answer, he replied that he would wait in the corridors leading to the lounge because I had most certainly some foreign currency he would gladly agree to accept! Faced with such arrogance and shamelessness I became slightly irritated and he stopped bothering me. There really are no small profits in Burundi!

My Visits in the Country Side

My first visit to the south along the shores of Lake Tanganyika towards Rumongue in the direction of the Tanzanian border created no issues since it was strictly private. Throughout the drive, where overloaded vehicles are commonplace, I could once again enjoy this series of small fishing villages squeezed between the lake and the steep mountains and the sandy beaches alternating with rocky shores that dip in the clear water of the lake. This heavenly setting, equivalent to or outmatching many tourist areas in the world has undoubtedly great potential just waiting to be exploited for the development of ecotourism. The exploitation of this potential should necessarily be selective because of the presence of crocodiles in rocky areas harboring dense aquatic vegetation. A modern hotel, the Tanganyika Blue Bay Resort, illustrates this potential. I stayed there for a weekend and highly appreciated the extraordinary charm of this site. Located 37 miles south of

Bujumbura towards Rumongue in front of a long beach of fine golden sand, this hotel is in my opinion one of the finest examples of what can be done with local materials without altering the original landscape while providing maximum safety for fanatics of aquatic activities. Let us hope that this beautiful resort can soon benefit from regular customers throughout the year. A more sustainable and secure environment is certainly one of the prerequisites for achieving this goal.

Overloaded truck on the road to Rumongue

Tanganyika Blue Bay Resort

Tanganyika Blue Bay Resort

The Blue Bay Resort – Finalizing my book

My other trips within the country have unfortunately proven to be more complex than I thought for administrative reasons on the one hand, and security on the other. From an administrative standpoint, everything appeared to me highly centralized and bureaucratic. Regarding security, I had many difficulties separating the draconian directives from the United Nations or the U.S. Embassy and the statements made by Burundians I would meet. These last ones were usually unanimous in declaring that security throughout the country was relatively good, at least for day trips.

My visit to Teza. Upon my arrival in Bujumbura, I had contacted the administrative services of the country's state-run Tea Board (Office du Thé du Burundi, OTB) to make my visit with possibly one of the managers of these services. However, to schedule my visit to the plantation where I worked for seven years, I ran into an administration of another time that would discourage many potential visitors. Indeed, in my contacts I remained at the level of the secretary office. The secretary was closed to all dialogues. Omnipotent, she said that a visit to Teza must necessarily be official because no one would see me otherwise. She therefore asked me to write a letter of request for a visit to the Tea Board management justifying the reasons for my visit. She also insisted that I put my seal on the letter! I requested to meet with the director to explain verbally my background and purpose of my visit and highlight the limited time available to me in Burundi. The omnipotent secretary who argued that I had to comply with the administrative circuit rejected my demand and told me to wait until someone contacted me. As for the seal to be affixed to my letter, the secretary finally acknowledged that not everyone has a seal and therefore it would not be necessary in my case since I was on a private "mission." Therefore, I submitted my letter of request to visit without obtaining details as to the response time because, of course the manager was busy. After five days, despite my phone calls and subsequent visits, the answer was always waiting. Infuriated by this administrative inefficiency and slowness, I decided to go through parallel circuits to complete my visit. As for potential security problems, I had to assess them by collecting opinions and feedback from the private sector, as well as international organizations before making my decision to visit or not visit the plantation. Indeed, Teza was still considered a very sensitive and risky area because it is on the edge of the forest of Kibira where armed gangs have taken refuge after the elections in June 2010. I had the option to follow the stringent and required recommendations for travel issued by the United Nations or the U.S. Embassy. The United Nations suggests that any trip within Burundi by staff of international institutions adhering to the instructions of the United Nations, like the World Bank, had to be done with an armed escort. As for the U.S. Embassy, the Consular Affairs Office of the State Department the United States issued shortly before my visit in early November 2010 further instructions for trips in Burundi limiting the movement of its staff to a perimeter of 18 miles around the capital and requiring prior authorization for any travel outside of this limit. All night trips were strictly discouraged and all drives after midnight within Bujumbura were also disapproved. Strict compliance with these requirements would have probably forced me to stay in Bujumbura, which was obviously not the purpose of my trip in Burundi. I could also override these measures by doing the best assessment of the potential risks. Despite recent threats made against staff of Teza, I opted for the latter because I thought that the military garrison stationed at Teza would guarantee some security at least during the daytime and that no incidents had been reported recently.

On a sunny Sunday, I went up to see the Teza tea plantation where I started my career in late 1963. I was accompanied by two Burundian acquaintances. One of them was working with the small-scale tea farmers[56] near Teza and was well known by the staff of the plantation. I was first struck by the quality of the roads leading up to Bugarama and beyond. This is actually only half a surprise since the President and several of his ministers are from the north and the highway I was taking continues towards the north and to Rwanda and is therefore highly strategic. When I arrived at Bugarama, which marks the beginning of the Congo-Nile crest, I was surprised by the dramatic changes rendering Bugarama unrecognizable. Indeed, twenty years ago, there were only a few vegetable stalls characterizing this important intersection between the northern axis or "Route Nationale" No. 1, leading to Rwanda and the one leading to Gitega, the second largest city. They had significantly expanded. The intersection was also the seat of an outbreak of various constructions, most of them providing light snacks making it a pivotal stopping point for motorists and truck drivers. Then I drove through the last 9 miles of paved road before taking the dirt track leading to the plantation. I was struck by the extent of deforestation on both sides of the road and by a significant improvement of habitat. The huts and houses with straw roofs that I knew had given way to adobe buildings topped by a tin roof. This development was for me an undeniable clue showing that the industrial and small-holders tea

---

[56] Small-scale tea farmers account for about 80% of tea production.

production introduced in 1963 in this area allowed farmers to increase their living standards by having steady income, which is not the case with annual crop cultures more subject to climatic and price fluctuations. All our work has not been in vain.

As for the visit itself, it allowed me to live an intense emotional moment. I scrutinized the faces around me in search for familiar and friendly features. To my surprise, I saw workers I knew some 35 years ago! Looking for memories, I wandered the empty rooms of our old cottage. Only walls and a roof remained of it. In this dilapidated cottage, there are so many memories. Then I went into our old house where we shared joys and tragedies that cannot be forgotten. When I came back through the garage, my heart tightened up. Indeed, it is through this garage that the column of murderers went to kill my agronomist next door. They assassinated him because he was Tutsi. This garage will forever be the silent witness of the tragic events of October 1965. I also found the plantation as I had left it in 1970. The 134 acres burned in 1996 by the insurgent movement during the civil war had been replanted, and the extensive damage that was caused to the factory during the same war had been repaired. Additionally, there is now a monument erected at the entrance of the factory to commemorate the brutal death of 117 Tutsis killed by rebels during the same year. I was deeply moved by this targeting killing because it reminded me of the sinister memories of 1965 and the massacre of Tutsis that occurred at exactly the same place. These employees, because of their Tutsi appurtenance, were also massacred. Unfortunately, they have not been entitled to remembrance. It is certainly not too late to right this wrong. The events unfortunately reoccurred as if Teza could not break away from these images of beauty and hell, these images of joys and sorrows that characterize it.

Our old cottage in the foreground

The "living room" of our cottage and the entrance to our "bedroom"

The plantation

The plantation

The plantation

A tea plant pruned

Memorial stone of the 1996 massacres

A historic homecoming to our former house

In the living room of our former house

The morbid garage and the house of my late agronomist in the background

A sad memory - The neighbor house of my agronomist

It is equally difficult to predict what the future holds because the Kibira forest that borders the plantation is unfortunately a perfect sanctuary for any rebel movement. Currently, working conditions are regrettably not optimal and I had confirmation that threats had been made shortly before my arrival against staff. For these reasons, the families of staff no longer live on the site of the plantation. The military presence near the plantation and at the top of Mount Teza, a strategic point overlooking the Kibira forest where a whole garrison is based, is certainly somewhat reassuring but also indicates that security problems are far from being resolved. Back in Bujumbura, I reconnected with the administrative services of OTB who had been so instrumental in planning my visit to Teza. I told them I had made my visit without permission and that I was received with open arms, contrary to what had been suggested. The secretary remained unmoved. A few days later, I learned from an acquaintance that the director had finally reviewed my application and then, hearing that my visit had already taken place, he classified my file without further action.

My visit to the Imbo plain. I also travelled to the Imbo plain to visit the ISABU agricultural research station where I worked from 1971 to 1974. Unlike the administrative difficulties that I encountered for visiting Teza, the manager of the station whom I met in the ISABU office in Bujumbura was extremely cooperative. We were able to make the trip without the indispensible mission order. As for safety, I faced the same dilemma that was posed for my trip to Teza. The situation was somewhat more complex. Indeed, serious incidents involving the deaths of several workers at a sugar factory near the Imbo Station had occurred two months earlier. These murders took place in the marshes of Rukoko, near the Ruzizi River along the Congolese border. According to government sources, these violent attacks were the work of unknown gunmen. This qualifier seems to hide a more disturbing reality as we will see later. Since the situation was now under control according to the authorities, I went ahead and decided to make the trip. Along the way, after leaving on our left the road going to the airfield, I especially enjoyed riding on a paved road instead of that dusty dirt road full of potholes that I drove daily 40 years ago. According to various reports, the improvement of the road network has clearly improved across a large part of the country. More striking, however, are the many tombs that line both sides of the road for about 3 miles and which document the atrocities of the recent civil war. However, the dead are not mixed. Dignitaries and senior government officials are buried separately and are clearly visible along the road. As for the poor, they are buried further within the natural park established by the government. Once at the station, I was taken aback by its dilapidated status. The buildings were neglected and in ruins, and weeds had taken over and invaded what was in the early 1970's a flourishing experimental agricultural research station. The civil war and the lack of financial resources that came from it have affected and unfortunately still affect the operations. Four years of efforts have been wiped out. Before returning to Bujumbura, the station manager suddenly asked me if I wanted to see the son of my former agronomist murdered in Teza during the events of October 1965. I immediately understood the importance of this meeting even though neither he, who was three years old at the time of the tragic death of his father, nor I knew one another. Our reunion was moving but discrete. Neither he nor I discussed the events of October 1965. However, I think it was important for the son of my ex-colleague to see me, since I am the only witness of this terrible tragedy that befell his family. In this meeting, I hope I participated in bringing closure in what has been a dark period of his existence.

On the way back, we met a group of workers maintaining the dirt road. I was struck by an interpellation concerning me, which tells a lot about the frequency of visits of foreigners. Indeed, I once more heard the name *Umuzungu,* which I heard during my first contacts with workers from Teza 47 years ago. In other words, the presence of a white person in this area does not seem frequent anymore. Then, continuing our trip, I asked my driver what he thought of the security problems in the plain. He told me cynically that it is quite possible that within this large group of workers we just crossed some could be responsible for the murders committed two months earlier at Rukoko! Scary!

On my way back to Bujumbura

Issues of the Return of Refugees

Since the independence in 1962, Burundi has gone through several coups, three genocides (1965, 1972 and 1988) and 13 years of civil war (from 1993 to 2006). These dark events were mainly caused by ethnic and political feuds. The death toll would exceed half a million in a population of about eight and a half million inhabitants, while hundreds of thousands fled to neighboring countries. These refugees are gradually coming back to Burundi without any guarantee to have their land and houses being returned to them, which poses a serious problem of reintegration. The sad reality is that there are currently very few families in Burundi that are unaffected by the war, genocides or life in refugee camps. At the hotel where I resided during my stay, I had the opportunity to speak with a 20-year-old Tutsi orphan who worked at the restaurant. He told me that his parents and several family members were murdered during the civil war when he was just six years old and that his outlook on life had changed since that tragic event. He said that the events related to the murder of his parents constantly haunt his dreams. He added that it is not the taste for life that he had lost but the trust in life. However, he kept his hope in starting college one day. I hope his wish will materialize and that young people in a situation similar to his can have access to the education, college-level or others, they aspire to receive so that their trust in life comes back gradually and that hope is born again.

I also spoke with a couple with modest incomes who were parents of six children, whose oldest is over twenty years old. To this already large family were added ten children orphaned since the civil war and whose parents had some kinship with this couple. This entire little world lives under the same roof of a modest home. These two cases are unfortunately not atypical, but are instead representative of a country torn for too long by these ethnic conflicts. These orphans are entitled to a future and they need assistance if the opportunity arises. In other countries there are NGOs that care for and sponsor orphans and destitute children. I know that similar organizations also provide some assistance in Burundi. For example, I like to mention the work undertaken by Dr. Deo Niyizonkiza who founded in his hometown of Kigutu[57] in 2006 the clinic Village Health Works, which is based on the concept of community-driven development. Regrettably, I did not have the opportunity during my stay to identify or analyze the actions taken by these organizations. The work of reconstruction of Burundi is a long-term venture and I hope that I may have one day the opportunity to bring my modest stone to the construction of this building.

Security Issues

Two other factors are grafted to the issues covered above. The first is the reintegration into everyday life of former rebels, including some of the 9,000 child soldiers or about one quarter of the old Hutu rebel force during the civil war, who have not been

---

[57] See Kidder, Tracy. *Op. cit.* and the site
<https://www.villagehealthworks.org/> (Accessed 12/28/2011).

hired by the army, the traffic police, or the private sector. These former rebels are theoretically disarmed but many sources state the contrary. They have received the equivalent of five hundred U.S. dollars paid in four quarterly installments to start a lucrative business other than war and crime. Armed or disarmed, this changes nothing to the issue of purchasing weapons. Indeed, several sources confirmed that it is extremely easy to obtain a weapon in Burundi at prices defying all competition, since an automatic weapon is trading at around two hundred dollars. I came across a former child soldier while I was lying at the beach in Bujumbura. There, a young guy approached me curious to know what I was doing alone on the beach. We started chatting for quite a while and after half an hour, he told me that he was a former child soldier. I was stunned and listened to him. He told me that he had lost his parents at the beginning of the civil war while he was thirteen years old. He then decided to take up arms to fight the Tutsi army. At the end of the war, he could not find any job nor did he get any aid. Yet, he has to support four brothers and sisters. He sadly told me that there is no hope for him, but that while he was in the bush life was so easy because he could easily live by plundering. He wonders, like many of his former child soldier acquaintances, if they will continue to live in peace and poverty or join rebels who promise them the spoils of war. The second factor was the decision made by seven political parties consisting of former rebels to withdraw from the sixteen that participated in the last electoral process. These rebels seem to have gone back to the bushes, some in the Rukoko marshes, as mentioned above, and others in the Kibira forest. Their leaders have gone underground and some are abroad.

The months before my arrival have also seen an upsurge of fighting between the military and small armed groups as well as attacks on civilians. In particular, a deadly attack took place in September 2010 about 19 miles northwest of the capital, while at the end of October 2010 some fighting took place in the eastern part of the capital. In Bujumbura, the mood is quite somber today. These attacks occurred after the release of a high-profile spokesperson for the army who stated that security was total and denied the existence of any rebel group in the making. At the end of 2010, the level of security in Burundi was actually ranked three out of five by the United Nations. This level of security can be a serious constraint to any development activity and all foreign investment in Burundi. The political situation was therefore uncertain when I visited; political opponents continued to be arrested, while journalists I met were struggling to do their job objectively. More and more Burundians with whom I had the opportunity to discuss with are also convinced that even if there has been no formal statement to date, a new rebellion is taking shape in the Rukoko marshes in the west and the Kibira forest in the north. However, this possibility continues to be denied by the political and military authorities that ensure that these groups are "groups of unidentified villains they are fighting off."[58]

---

[58] Radio France International. *Burundi - Une nouvelle rébellion refait surface au Burundi* [A new rebellion resurfaces in Burundi]. Septembre 2010.

XIII. EPILOGUE

September 15, 2010. His Excellency (HE), Pierre Nkurunziza, was sworn in his second Presidential term for the state of Burundi and then he was awarded the Peace Prize "Beaming Star of Africa" by the International Foundation of Unity.[59]

In the speech HE gave on this occasion, [60] it is worth noting several points indicating the progress made by Burundi in the fields of peace building, democracy and development. HE first pointed out that the first term he had just completed was a milestone in political life in Burundi. Indeed, for the first time in Burundi's history a democratically elected President was able to complete its mandate, as the previous democratically elected Presidents were all assassinated while in office. The second point relates to the smooth integration of former combatants in the national defense and security. The success of this integration has enabled Burundi to be chosen as a model in the consolidation of peace by the United Nations Security Council. Given the progress made by the government of Burundi for peace, stability and development, the Council also decided to significantly reduce the United Nations's presence in Burundi starting January 1, 2011. The third point highlights the return of many Burundians who had taken refuge during the civil war in neighboring countries. HE also noted that while the war is over the development challenges remain enormous.

In fact, as I saw during my last trip, the challenges are enormous but not insurmountable. It is thus conceivable that the wisdom and sense of sharing take precedence over the sources of violence such as corruption, food insecurity, isolationism and refusal to live together. The sufferings and difficulties of Burundi's recent history clearly indicate that deeply entrenched unresolved oppositions can lead, in certain situations, to explosions of violence in which all sense of humanity seems to have disappeared. As a prominent Burundi journalist remarked, "People are tired of war, but they are

---

[59] "Étoile Rayonnante d'Afrique"
[60] See *Burundi Information.* September 15, 2010.

so poor. This kind of poverty can push people to provoke change." To experience true peace and work towards a new and peaceful coexistence, each nation needs to come to terms with itself. If we do not create in the hearts this strength of mind for reconciliation, the inner predisposition lacks the commitment to peace. Therefore, I firmly believe that the road of hope for Burundi will begin when there is a reduction in current disagreements between the government and parties that have recently separated from the electoral process. Then the security constraints that are a major obstacle to development will dissipate and the hope of a better future can be realized.

I left Burundi, this wonderful country I love so much, with the hope that the sad events that have devastated the country since independence do not reoccur and that Burundians can now live together as they lived long ago and better, if possible. For this wish to occur, I decided to write this book because I had an experience to share about the life of a family of expatriates in that distant country, and about my experience during subsequent visits. I wrote it because I also felt the intimate need to witness what I heard, saw and experienced to provide, I hope, my stone to a better understanding of indicators pointing to the destruction of the unity of a country. Indeed, what happened in Burundi and other countries where ethnic conflicts have been at least as devastating could happen tomorrow in any other country in the world, providing a fertile ground for extremists. In order for this dark tomorrow to go unfulfilled, we must remember that the unity in Burundi did not disappear in one day, that this disappearance required time and that the signs of the long descent into hell, which culminated in the recent thirteen-year civil war were already present during the attempted 1965 coup, which we witnessed but received little media coverage. It must also be remembered that the significant responsibility of the Belgian colonial power in the establishment of an ethnic divide in Burundi by favoring, during a forty-year administration, a small minority at the expense of the majority. This topic is heavily documented; I will not dwell unduly on the colonial history of Burundi. I also believe that the recent incidents in the Rukoko reserve[61] and in the Kibira forest should not be minimized by attributing them to groups of bandits. Can we speak of bandits while members of six parties decided to leave the electoral process and go into hiding with their weapons? I do not think so. The government should be transparent in its

---

[61] La réserve de la Rukoko. In Burundi Transparence.

communication with the media and the public and should pay greater attention to leading indicators of political destabilization. Finally, an attack on a bar in Gatumba near the capital of Bujumbura killed nearly 40 people and injured many others on September 18, 2011. We can only hope that this is an isolated case and not another step in the escalation of political violence. This attack should, however, not be underestimated. A Burundi friend of mine also recently confirmed that the security had deteriorated in the country. Therefore, more than ever, the government should open up a dialogue with armed dissidents. Indeed, only dialogues can overcome potential obstacles and provide a democratic solution of lasting peace in Burundi. That is why I think it was important for me to bring forth my testimony so that the pointers of destructive ideas may no longer propagate freely.

In the Land of Joys and Sorrows

ANNEX. LAKE TANGANYIKA

The Context

Lake Tanganyika borders Burundi along 93 miles and covers a total area of 12,700 square miles, which is approximately the same size as Belgium or the state of Maryland in the United States. The Burundian part represents about 8% of this area, with the remainder split between the Democratic Republic of Congo (45%), Tanzania (41%) and Zambia (6%). Formed during the Miocene about 20 million years ago, Lake Tanganyika is the oldest lake in the African Rift Valleys. Worldwide, it is the seventh lake by area and the second lake by depth after Lake Baikal in Russia. It reaches in places a depth of 4,708 feet, which is about 2,106 feet below the sea level! This lake is the largest reservoir of fresh water in Africa. Many tributaries, the most important one being the Ruzizi River, which drains Lake Kivu and the Malagarazi River, which drains western Tanzania, feed it. On the left edge of Lake Tanganyika is its outlet, the Lukuga River.

Wildlife

Lake Tanganyika contains a particularly rich and diversified hallieutic fauna in the benthic and coastal areas.[62] This diversity is actually similar to the one encountered in oceans. Among the fauna represented are nearly 300 species including Cichlids (*Neolamprologus, Paleolamprologus, Altolamprologus, Xenotilapia, Julidochromis, Telmatochromis, Tropheus* and *Petrochromis*), Actinopterygii (*Stolothrissa* and *Limnothrissa*) and Cyprinodontiformes (*Lamprichthys*). About two-thirds of these fishes are endemic. This rich fauna is an irresistible attraction to those fond of underwater exploration. Without going into too

---

[62] Lévêque, Christian; Paugy, Didier. *Les poissons des eaux continentales africaines : diversité, écologie, utilisation par l'homme*. [Fishes from African Inland Waters: Diversity, Ecology, Human Uses].

specific details, I will distinguish the two communities that are most accessible to divers and allow me to better share with the reader the beautiful dives I have been fortunate enough to make in this lake.

The Pelagic Community

The pelagic community is mainly composed of six endemic species including two Clupeidae, the Lake Tanganyika sprat (*Stolothrissa tanganicae*) and the Lake Tanganyika sardine (*Limnothrissa miodon*). They occupy the pelagic zone where they live in shoals and consume phytoplankton and zooplankton. Both are major pelagic biomasses of the lake and an important resource for fishermen and for the feeding of the population. They also serve as food for predators belonging to the gender Lates or Nile perch (*Lates niloticus*). The *Lates* originates from Ethiopia and is mistakenly called "captain." It can reach a length of more than 6.5 feet and is one of the most interesting targets for industrial and artisanal lake fishing. We also note the presence of tilapias introduced into the Congo in 1950 and of the African catfish or Clarias, also known as Silures.

Sublittoral and Littoral Communities

Sublittoral and littoral communities live along the coast at a depth not exceeding 130 feet where Cichlids are dominant. Most of the littoral zone is steep and rocky, with sand beaches, gravel beaches and river mouths here and there. Compared to the pelagic zone, species-poor, the coastal fish communities are much richer and have more complex structures. Among the Cichlids, the lamprologini group contains the most species and may constitute over 50% of species in the coastal community. Many catfish live there. In the crevices offered by the rocky environment, there is another vertebrate, the dreaded aquatic naja (*Boulengerina annulata stormsi*), also known as water cobra, one of the few species of swimmer snakes, who eat fish. The water cobra is a reptile adapted to underwater life, just like the sea snakes of coral reefs. While very comfortable in water, it is much less on earth.[63]

---

[63] Chippaux, Jean-Philippe. *Les serpents d'Afrique occidentale et centrale.* [Snakes from Western and Central Africa]

All divers because of its lethal bite fear it. Finally, in addition to this diverse wildlife, the lake is also home to species generally characteristic of marine life such as sponges, jellyfish and crustaceans.

Aquatic and Terrestrial Species

Crocodiles (*Crocodylus niloticus* and *Crocodylus cataphractus*) and hippopotamus (*Hippopotamus amphibious*) are particularly common. The crocodiles are usually found along the shores and in estuaries. Along the estuary of the Ruzizi River, they are often seen open-mouthed resting on the banks. Contrary to what one might think that position is not at all aggressive--it is a ventilation system allowing better heat loss. Crocodiles are extremely aggressive during the breeding season and cause many accidents in the lake. Hippos are very frequent along the banks and in open water. Finally, the fascinating and extremely poisonous puffer fish (Tetraodon mbu) also inhabit the entrance of estuaries. This fish is a poor swimmer but it is characterized by an extraordinary development of the skeleton and a physiological system allowing it to quickly inflate by swallowing air or water when it feels threatened. With this mechanism of swelling, whose explanation was suggested only recently in 1994 and 1995 (Brainerd and Wainwright), they can double in volume.

In the Land of Joys and Sorrows

Bibliography

Authors

Baghdadi, Ilhem; Harborne, Richard; Rajadel, Tania (Editors). *Rompre le cercle vicieux. Une stratégie pour promouvoir la croissance dans un milieu rural sensible aux conflits au Burundi.* World Bank Working Papers, 2008.

Braeckman, Colette. *Terreur africaine. Burundi, Rwanda, Zaïre: les racines de la violence.* Fayard, 1996.

Capecchi, Bernard. *Teza, une grande exploitation théière au Burundi.* Les cahiers d'Outre-Mer: revue de géographie de Bordeaux et de l'Atlantique. Volume 29 #115 1976. pp. 271-301.

Chippaux, Jean-Philippe. *Les serpents d'Afrique occidentale et centrale.* Ird Orstom, 2006.

Chrétien, Jean-Pierre; Dupaquier, Jean-François. *Burundi 1972, au bord des génocides.* Karthala, 2007.

Duren, A., Gillet, H. *Notions élémentaires d'hygiène tropicale à l'usage des habitants du Congo Belge.* 4e ed. Bruxelles: IMIFI, 1957.

Eggers, Ellen K. *Historical Dictionary of Burundi.* Third ed. Lanham, Maryland: Scarecrow Press, 2006.

Emerson, Rupert. 'The Fate of Human Rights in the Third World,' *World Politics* 27, (1975).

Gates, Henry Louis (Editor). *Africana: The Encyclopedia of the African and African American Experience.* New York: Basic Civitas Books, 1999. p. 338

Hallet, Jean-Pierre. *Congo Kitabu*. Fawcett Crest Books; Unabridged edition (1967).

Hasley, Carr Rosamond. *Le pays aux mille collines: ma vie au Rwanda*. Paris: Editions Payot et Rivages, 2004.

Inganji, Ephrem. *Une jeunesse perdue dans un abattoir d'hommes*. L'Harmattan, 2008.

Kay, Reginald. *"Burundi since the Genocide", Report tracing the Consequences of the 1972 Genocide*. London: Minority Rights Group Report no. 20, 1987.

Kidder, Tracy. *Strength in What Remains: A Journey of Remembrance and Forgiveness*. New York: Random House, 2009.

Krueger, Ambassador Robert; Tobin Krueger, Kathleen. *From Bloodshed to Hope in Burundi. Our Embassy Years during Genocide*. University of Texas Press, 2007.

Lemarchand, René et Martin David. *"Selective Genocide in Burundi", Report on the 1972 genocide*. London: Minority Rights Group Report no. 20, 1974.

Lemarchand, René. *Burundi Ethnic Conflict and Genocide*. Washington, D.C.: Woodrow Wilson Center Press, 1996.

Lemarchand, René. *Burundi's Endangered Transition. Fast Country Risk Profile, Burundi*. Bern, 2006.

Lévêque, Christian et Paugy, Didier. *Les poissons des eaux continentales africaines: diversité, écologie, utilisation par l'homme*. Paris: IRD, 1999.

Manirakiza, Marc. *Burundi: De la révolution au régionalisme (1966-1976)*. Paris; Bruxelles: Le Mât de Misaine, 1992.

Manirakiza, Marc. *La fin de la monarchie burundaise (1962-1966)*. Paris; Bruxelles: Le Mât de Misaine, 1990.

MPD (Mouvement pour la paix au Burundi). Mémorandum sur les massacres répétitifs des Hutu au Burundi. Appel à la conscience mondiale, Bujumbura, 1992.

Nemry, Claude. *Les Tambours du Rwanda*. Paris: l'Harmattan, 2001.

Ntampaka, Charles. *La question foncière au Burundi. Implications pour le retour des réfugiés, la consolidation de la paix et le développement rural*. Rome: F.A.O., 2006.

O'Shea, Mark; Halliday, Tim. *Reptiles and Amphibians*. DK Pub, 2002.

Ricœur, Paul. *La mémoire, l'histoire, l'oubli*. Seuil, 2000.

Rwagasore, Prince Louis. Imprimerie du Royaume du Burundi.

Saitoti, Tepilit Ole. *The worlds of a Maasai Warrior*. University of California Press, 1986 (1988 printing).

Uvin, Peter. *Life after Violence. A people's Story of Burundi*. London; New York: Zed, 2009.

Other Sources

Burundi Information. *Discours de SE le Président Pierre NKURUNZIZA à l'occasion de la remise du prix de la paix « Etoile Rayonnant d'Afrique » lui décerné par la Fondation Internationale de l'Unité*. Le 15 septembre 2010 par Jean-Claude Mubisharukanywa. Available at: <http://www.burundi-info.com/spip.php?article1343>. (Last accessed 2/13/2012)

De Coninck, Michèle. *Mes années au Burundi*. Available at: <http://madamoiselle-michere.skynetblogs.be/>. (Last accessed 2/13/2012).

ICG. Burundi: Democracy and Peace at Risk, Africa Report N°120, Nov 30, 2006.

ICG. Burundi: Finalizing Peace with the FNL, Africa Report N°131, Aug 28, 2007.

ICG. Burundi: To Integrate the FNL Successfully, Africa Briefing N°63, 30 Jul 2009.

IMF. Burundi: Selected Issues and Statistical Appendix. IMF Country Report No 06/307. Aug 2006.

Institut des Sciences Agronomiques du Burundi. Rapport Annuel 1970.

La réserve de la Rukoko. In Burundi Transparence (Source: AFP) [online], 15 September 2010 Available at: <http://www.burunditransparence.org/operation_militaire_rukoko.html>. (Last accessed 2/13/2012).

Radio France International. *Burundi - Une nouvelle rébellion refait surface au Burundi*. September 2010 [online].

Swisspeace. "Burundi's Endangered Transition," FAST Country Risk Profile. Paper No. 5. Bonn, Switzerland: Swisspeace Foundation, 2006. Available at: <http://www.rfi.fr/afrique/20100912-une-nouvelle-rebellion-refait-surface-burundi> (Last accessed 2/13/2012)

The World Bank; Burundi - Data & Statistics. Burundi at a glance. February 25, 2011. Available at: <http://devdata.worldbank.org/AAG/bdi_aag.pdf> (Last accessed 2/13/2012).

Transparency International. Corruption index 2010. Report of October 28, 2010.

U.S. Department Of State. Bureau of Consular Affairs. *Travel Warning for Burundi*. Notice of June 1, 2011 replacing the notice of November 4, 2010. Available at: <http://travel.state.gov/travel/cis_pa_tw/tw/tw_2122.html> (Last accessed 2/13/2012)

Wikipedia – Crocodile, October 2011 [on line], Available at: <http://en.wikipedia.org/> (Last accessed 2/13/2012)

Wikipedia – Gustave (crocodile), September 2011 [on line], Available at: <http://en.wikipedia.org/> (Last accessed 2/13/2012)

Wikipedia – Origins of Tutsi and Hutu [on line], Available at: <http://en.wikipedia.org/> (Last accessed 2/13/2012)

Bibliography

In the Land of Joys and Sorrows

Editions Innovations and Information

Books published

In French

Antoine-Ganga, Dieudonné. *Si Bacongo m'était conté*. 2011.
Antoine-Ganga, Dieudonné. *Grand-père, parle-nous du peuple koongo*. 2010.
Serejski, Eric. *Le Kama Sutra chinois. Sexualité et dysfonctions sexuelles*. 2007.
Serejski, Ivar. *Au pays des joies et des drames – Notre vie au Burundi*. 2012.

In English

Serejski, Eric. *The Jesuits Driven Away from Masonry and Their Dagger Shattered by Freemasons*. Translation from *Les Jésuites chassés de la Maçonnerie et leur poignard brisé par les Maçons* (1788) par Nicholas de Bonneville. 2011.
Serejski, Eric. *The Chinese Kama Sutra. Sexuality and Sexual Dysfunctions in Ancient China*. Translation from Chinese. 2007
Serejski, Eric. *Shan Hai Jing*. Volume 1 - *The Classics of Mountains*. Translation from Chinese. 2010.

Ebooks published

In French

Serejski, Ivar. *Au pays des joies et des drames – Notre vie au Burundi*. 2012.

In English

Serejski, Eric. *The Jesuits Driven Away from Masonry and Their Dagger Shattered by Freemasons*. Translation from *Les Jésuites chassés de la Maçonnerie et leur poignard brisé par les Maçons* (1788) par Nicholas de Bonneville. 2011.
Serejski, Eric. *Shan Hai Jing*. Volume 1 - *The Classics of Mountains*. Translation from Chinese. 2010.

www.ingramcontent.com/pod-product-compliance
Lightning Source LLC
Chambersburg PA
CBHW032045150426
43194CB00006B/429